CW01238995

FRANCIS FRITH'S

HARROGATE - A HISTORY AND CELEBRATION

THE FRANCIS FRITH COLLECTION

www.francisfrith.com

HARROGATE

A HISTORY AND CELEBRATION OF THE TOWN

ROLY SMITH

Produced by The Francis Frith Collection

www.francisfrith.com

First published in the United Kingdom in 2004 by
The Francis Frith Collection®

Hardback Edition 2004 ISBN 1-90493-830-2
Paperback Edition 2012 ISBN 978-1-84589-635-5

Text and Design copyright © The Francis Frith Collection®
Photographs copyright © The Francis Frith Collection

The Frith photographs and the Frith logo are reproduced under licence from Heritage Photographic Resources Ltd, the owners of the Frith archive and trademarks

All rights reserved. No photograph in this publication may be sold to a third party other than in the original form of this publication, or framed for sale to a third party.
No parts of this publication may be reproduced, stored in a retrieval system, or transmitted, in any form, or by any means, electronic, mechanical, photocopying, recording or otherwise, without the prior permission of the publishers and copyright holder.

British Library Cataloguing in Publication Data

Harrogate - A History and Celebration of the Town
Roly Smith

The Francis Frith Collection®
Oakley Business Park, Wylye Road,
Dinton, Wiltshire SP3 5EU
Tel: +44 (0) 1722 716 376
Email: info@francisfrith.co.uk
www.francisfrith.com

Printed and bound in Great Britain
Contains material sourced from responsibly managed forests

Front Cover: **HARROGATE, ROYAL PUMP ROOM 1911**
63522t

Additional photographs by John Morrison.
Domesday extract used in timeline by kind permission of
Alecto Historical Editions, www.domesdaybook.org.
Aerial photographs reproduced under licence from
Simmons Aerofilms Limited.
Historical Ordnance Survey maps reproduced under licence from
Homecheck.co.uk

The colour-tinting in this book is for illustrative purposes only, and is not intended to be historically accurate

AS WITH ANY HISTORICAL DATABASE, THE FRANCIS FRITH ARCHIVE IS CONSTANTLY BEING CORRECTED AND IMPROVED, AND THE PUBLISHERS WOULD WELCOME INFORMATION ON OMISSIONS OR INACCURACIES

Contents

6   Timeline

8   Chapter 1 : Early History

22   Chapter 2 : The Spa Years

40   Chapter 3 : Victorian Harrogate

68   Chapter 4 : The Twentieth Century

102   Chapter 5 : Harrogate Today

117   Acknowledgements, Dedication and Bibliography

121   Free Mounted Print Offer

HARROGATE, FROM THE AIR 1933 AF43175

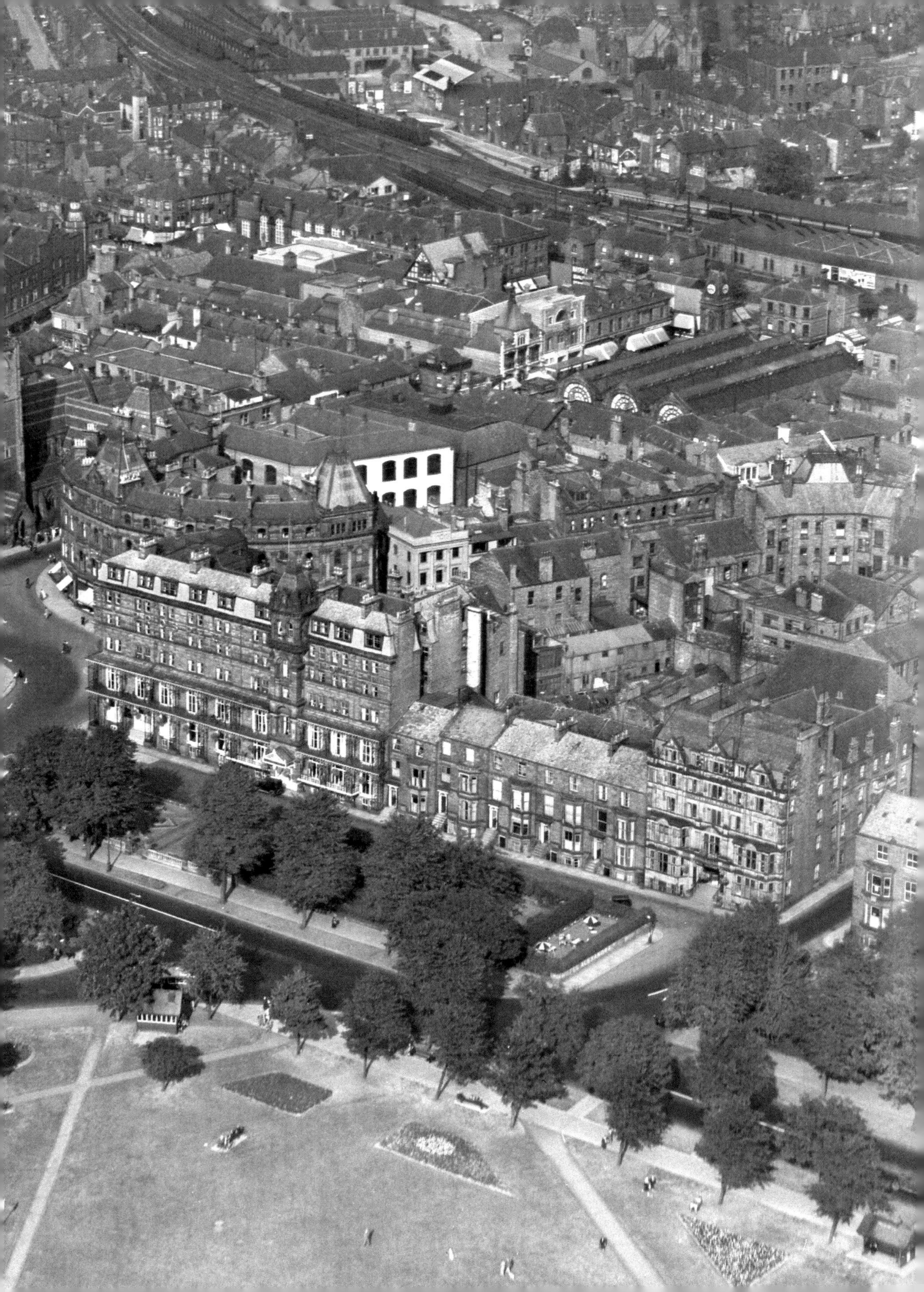

HARROGATE – *a history and celebration of the town*

Historical Timeline for Harrogate

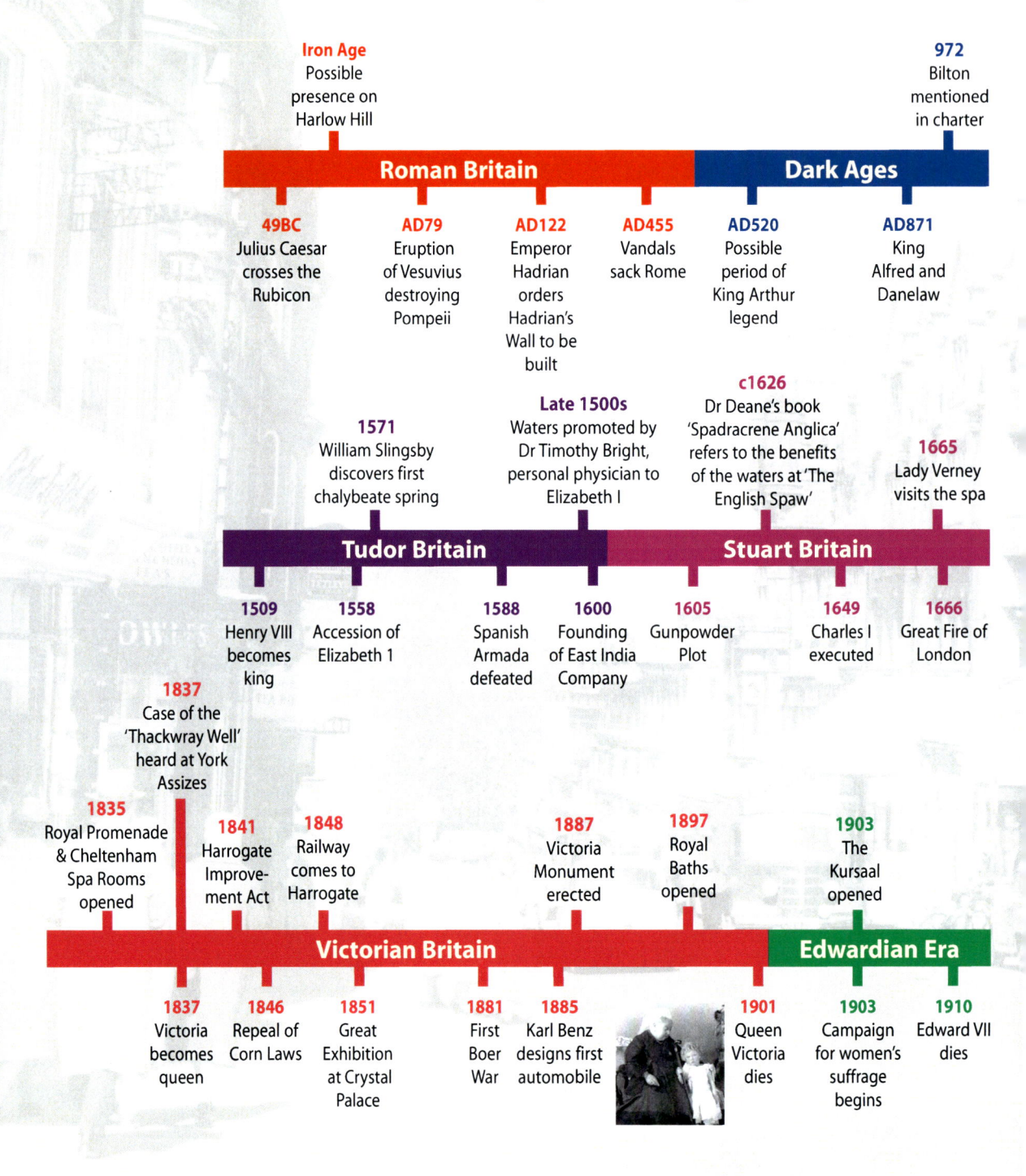

Iron Age — Possible presence on Harlow Hill

972 — Bilton mentioned in charter

Roman Britain | Dark Ages

49BC — Julius Caesar crosses the Rubicon

AD79 — Eruption of Vesuvius destroying Pompeii

AD122 — Emperor Hadrian orders Hadrian's Wall to be built

AD455 — Vandals sack Rome

AD520 — Possible period of King Arthur legend

AD871 — King Alfred and Danelaw

1571 — William Slingsby discovers first chalybeate spring

Late 1500s — Waters promoted by Dr Timothy Bright, personal physician to Elizabeth I

c1626 — Dr Deane's book 'Spadracrene Anglica' refers to the benefits of the waters at 'The English Spaw'

1665 — Lady Verney visits the spa

Tudor Britain | Stuart Britain

1509 — Henry VIII becomes king

1558 — Accession of Elizabeth 1

1588 — Spanish Armada defeated

1600 — Founding of East India Company

1605 — Gunpowder Plot

1649 — Charles I executed

1666 — Great Fire of London

1837 — Case of the 'Thackwray Well' heard at York Assizes

1835 — Royal Promenade & Cheltenham Spa Rooms opened

1841 — Harrogate Improvement Act

1848 — Railway comes to Harrogate

1887 — Victoria Monument erected

1897 — Royal Baths opened

1903 — The Kursaal opened

Victorian Britain | Edwardian Era

1837 — Victoria becomes queen

1846 — Repeal of Corn Laws

1851 — Great Exhibition at Crystal Palace

1881 — First Boer War

1885 — Karl Benz designs first automobile

1901 — Queen Victoria dies

1903 — Campaign for women's suffrage begins

1910 — Edward VII dies

Middle Ages

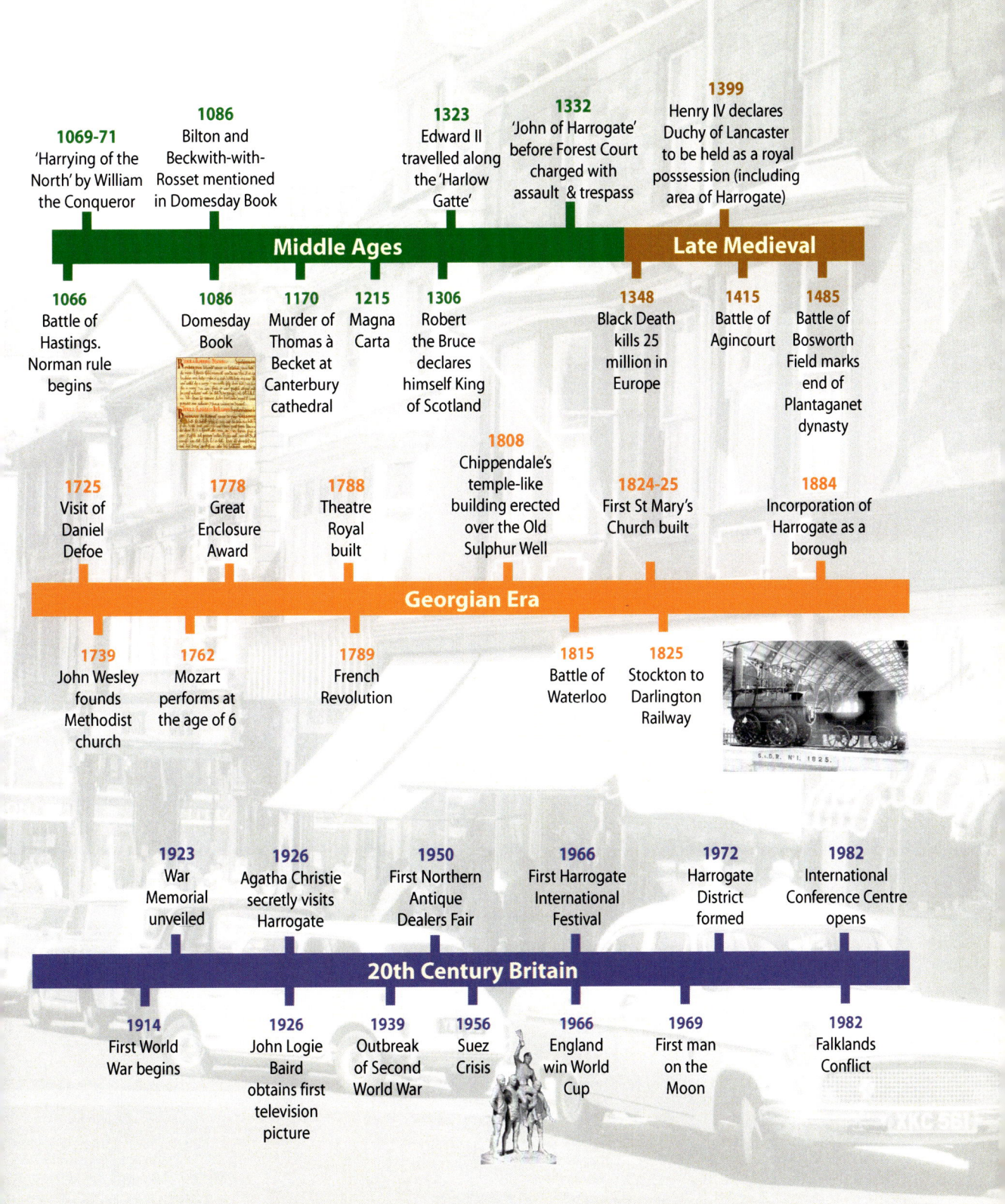

1069-71 'Harrying of the North' by William the Conqueror

1086 Bilton and Beckwith-with-Rosset mentioned in Domesday Book

1323 Edward II travelled along the 'Harlow Gatte'

1332 'John of Harrogate' before Forest Court charged with assault & trespass

Late Medieval

1399 Henry IV declares Duchy of Lancaster to be held as a royal posssession (including area of Harrogate)

1066 Battle of Hastings. Norman rule begins

1086 Domesday Book

1170 Murder of Thomas à Becket at Canterbury cathedral

1215 Magna Carta

1306 Robert the Bruce declares himself King of Scotland

1348 Black Death kills 25 million in Europe

1415 Battle of Agincourt

1485 Battle of Bosworth Field marks end of Plantaganet dynasty

1725 Visit of Daniel Defoe

1778 Great Enclosure Award

1788 Theatre Royal built

1808 Chippendale's temple-like building erected over the Old Sulphur Well

1824-25 First St Mary's Church built

1884 Incorporation of Harrogate as a borough

Georgian Era

1739 John Wesley founds Methodist church

1762 Mozart performs at the age of 6

1789 French Revolution

1815 Battle of Waterloo

1825 Stockton to Darlington Railway

1923 War Memorial unveiled

1926 Agatha Christie secretly visits Harrogate

1950 First Northern Antique Dealers Fair

1966 First Harrogate International Festival

1972 Harrogate District formed

1982 International Conference Centre opens

20th Century Britain

1914 First World War begins

1926 John Logie Baird obtains first television picture

1939 Outbreak of Second World War

1956 Suez Crisis

1966 England win World Cup

1969 First man on the Moon

1982 Falklands Conflict

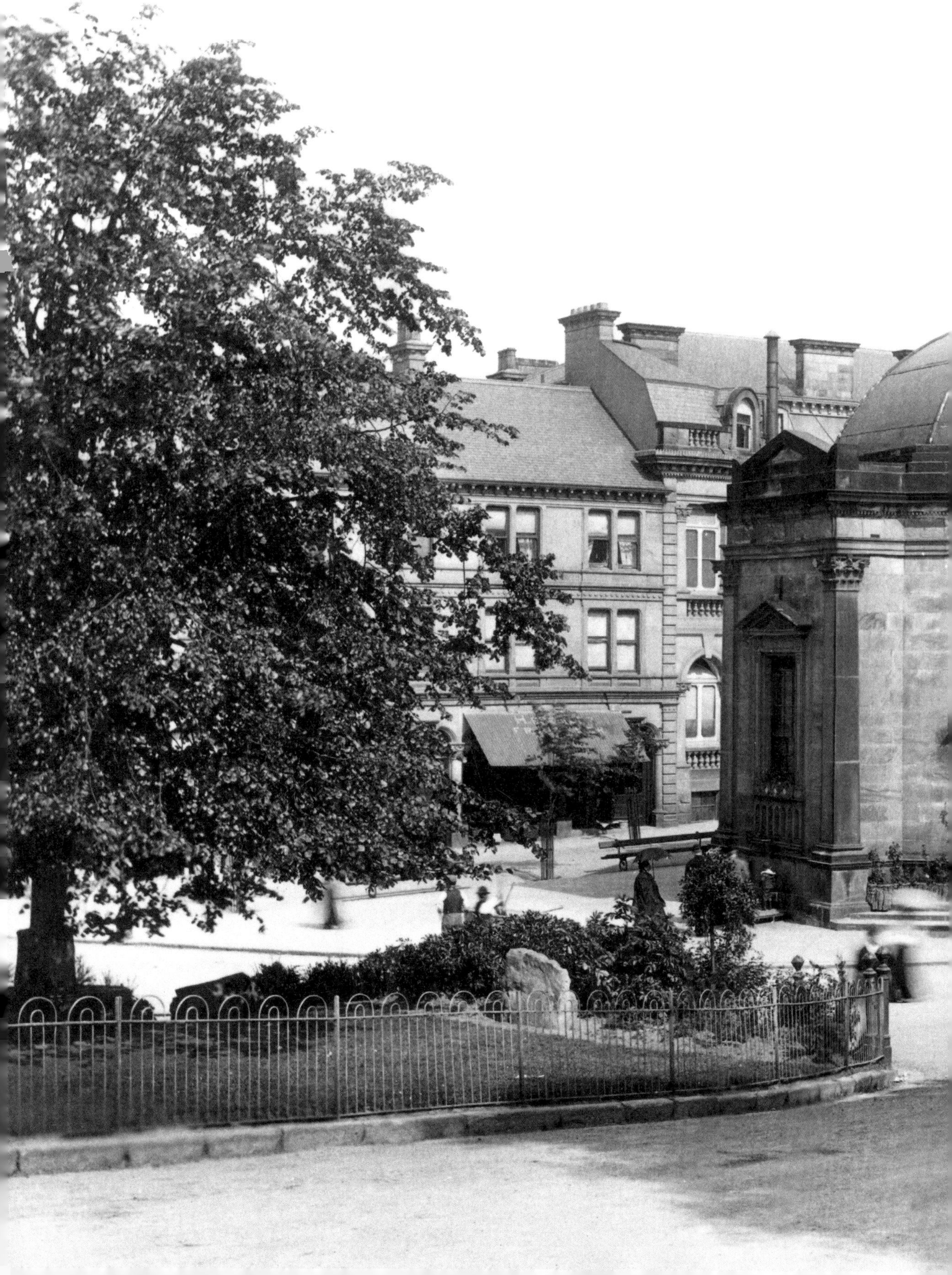

CHAPTER ONE

Early History

EXTERIOR OF THE PUMP ROOM 1853 ZZZ02013

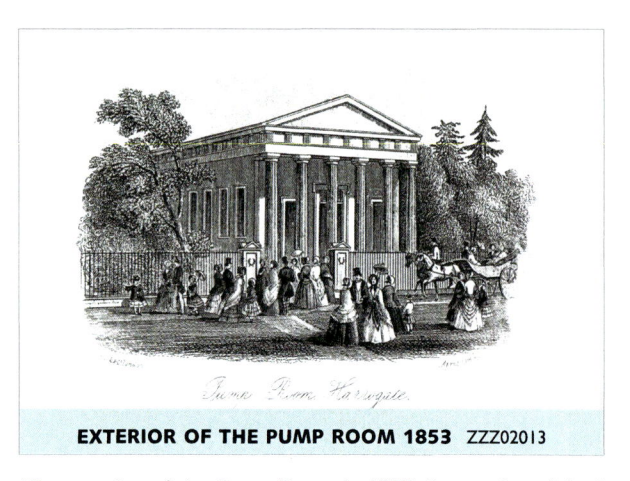

INTERIOR OF THE PUMP ROOM 1853 ZZZ02012

The exterior of the Pump Room in 1853. It was demolished in 1939.

MANY BRITISH SPA TOWNS - such as Bath and Buxton - can trace their origins back over 2,000 years to the Romans' predilection to hot springs and their love of bathing in them. But although Harrogate has a good claim to be Britain's greatest spa, there is no firm evidence that the Romans ever used the town's famous chalybeate and sulphur springs. On the map in his 1871 'History and Topography of Harrogate', William Grainge marks Roman camps at Horn Bank near Pannal and on Killinghall Moor, and also a Roman road running north-south between Catterick and Adel, which passed to the west of Harrogate close to Harlow Hill; but these have never been confirmed.

No one can know for sure who were the first people who settled on the higher ground above the southern banks of the River Nidd, opposite the ancient riverside settlement of Knaresborough, the site now known as Harrogate. The double-banked promontory fort of Bank Slack at Fewston, about seven miles west of Harrogate off the A59, certainly shows that there was an Iron Age presence in the region, and the circular enclosure on the high point of Harlow Hill (600ft/183m) closer to the town may also possibly have a prehistoric provenance. There are some vague mentions of a Dark Age battle in the vicinity of the hill, but again there is no conclusive archaeological evidence to prove it.

Certainly the prominent Harlow Hill seems to have been an important landmark, and the second element of its name, 'low', corresponds to the Old English 'hlaw' meaning 'hill' or 'burial mound', as it does in the many 'lows' of the Peak District, the 'howes' of the North York Moors, and the 'laws' of Scotland. Other Harlows, for example those in Essex and in Northumberland, were 'the mounds of the people' and a meeting place of the administrative hundred in early medieval times, but it is pure supposition to suggest that the same might also have applied to Harrogate's Harlow.

Early History

Harlow Hill

The heathy vegetation with scattered pine trees on Harlow Moor gives us a good idea of what the area now occupied by Harrogate may have looked like in prehistory, when the first people arrived in the area. Harlow Hill and Moor, to the west of the town centre, may well have seen the earliest human settlement in the area, and the circular boundary on Harlow Hill could possibly indicate an Iron Age enclosure. The picture shows the poppy-decorated crucifix war memorial on Harlow Moor.

THE WAR MEMORIAL AND HARLOW MOOR 1921 71666

The earliest evidence of human settlement that has yet been found in the area is the so-called Harrogate Hoard of spearheads dating from the Bronze Age which were uncovered at Bilton, to the north of the present town, in 1848. Bilton was founded in Anglo-Saxon times; the name means 'Billa's enclosure', and the first mention of any part of what is now Harrogate occurs when Bilton is referred to in an AD972 document detailing the territories of church lands belonging to Northumbria.

ARTIST'S IMPRESSION OF SAXON HOUSES F6015

The name of Harrogate continues to puzzle etymologists, as it has for many years. But what is certain is that it denotes an early settlement, probably dating from the days when the Norse raiders from across the North Sea were venturing into the Yorkshire dales. The local historian Malcolm Neesam suggests that the likelihood is that Harrogate was a 9th-century geographical place name for an area which later became settled. The neighbouring River Nidd certainly has an ancient Celtic name, which is thought to mean 'brilliant water', or perhaps what we might call today 'sparkling'.

According to Professor Eilert Ekwall in his 'Concise Oxford Dictionary of English Place Names', the second element of the name, 'gate', definitely comes from the Old Scandinavian 'gate' meaning 'road', perhaps used here in the North Country sense of 'a right of pasturage for cattle'. The first element, 'Harro', is more problematic, but Ekwall also links it to the neighbouring hilltop of Harlow, which he says means 'grey hill'. Thus Harrogate may mean 'the road to, or pasturage for cattle near, Harlow Hill'. Yet another interpretation is that Harlow ('here-low') means 'soldier's hill'; indeed, Grainge claims it to be the traditional site of an encampment used by Uther Pendragon, the father of King Arthur, in AD460, during that confusing and disturbed period after the departure of the Roman legions. However, there is no archaeological evidence to support such a claim.

There is no doubt that over the next few centuries Saxons, Angles, Danes and Norsemen gradually settled in the area of Yorkshire, leaving behind many of the village and town place names still in use in the locality today.

There can be no doubt either that the Harrogate area suffered (as did the rest of the north of England) under William the Conqueror's vicious 'Harrying of the North' in 1069-71, which followed a revolt in the north-east against the new Norman overlords imposed on the country following the Battle of Hastings. This was a deliberate and coldly-calculated campaign of genocide which left large areas of the countryside as wasteland - these were each later to be recorded in the Latin of the Domesday Book as 'wasta est'. Villages and towns were left in flames, and the streets were littered with the bodies of men, women and children. Within living memory of these horrific events, the chronicler Orderic Vitalis recorded the scene:

'In his anger he (William) commanded that all crops and herds, chattels and food of every kind should be brought together and burned to ashes with consuming fire, so that the whole region north of the Humber might be stripped of all means of sustenance. In consequence so serious a scarcity was felt in England, and

A NORMAN SHIP F6019

so terrible a famine fell upon the humble and defenceless population, that more than 100,000 Christian folk of both sexes, young and old alike, perished of hunger.'

Later, what is now Harrogate formed the central part of the Forest of Knaresborough, a royal hunting forest governed from the stronghold of Knaresborough Castle built on its hill above the River Nidd during the 12th century. It is strange that Knaresborough Forest was not mentioned in the Domesday Book of 1086, but it must have been established soon afterwards in the late 11th century. William I's great survey of his newly won kingdom does, however, contain references to land holdings in what was later to become Harrogate. The two hamlets of Bilton and Beckwith-with-Rossett, including Pannal, are mentioned, foreshadowing the later twin communities of High and Low Harrogate, a distinction which is still made more than nine centuries later.

The royal hunting preserve of the Forest of Knaresborough stretched westward from the town of Knaresborough across the Nidd as far as Thornthwaite (another Norse name) and Great Timble, to Swindon, nearly on the banks of the Wharfe to the south. In general terms, it was bounded by the rivers or streams of the Nidd, the Wharfe, the Crimple Beck and the Washburn. Included within the forest boundaries were enclosed parks such as Bilton Park and Haverah Park, granted by Henry II to William de Stuteville in 1173. Fodder from Haverah Park was reserved for horses in the royal stud, according to records from 1318-19 during the reign of Edward II.

A MEDIEVAL KNIGHT AND HIS LADY, FROM INGHAM CHURCH, NORFOLK F6018

Yet another interpretation of the name of Harrogate is that it might mean 'the road to Haverah', where the so-called John of Gaunt's Castle was probably only a hunting lodge - it was almost certainly used by Edward II when he was recorded as travelling along 'the Harlow Gatte' from Knaresborough in 1323.

The Scottish invasions of 1318 destroyed the town of Knaresborough, and the Scots then entered the royal forest, burning down the church at Pannal. Not everyone seems to have been opposed to the Scottish invasion, however, and an intriguing insight into those troubled times is an existing pardon for someone called William Snawe of Bilton for 'adhering to the Scots'.

A medieval hunting forest was not anything like what is popularly imagined as a forest today. There may well have been considerable tree cover, but a 'forest' in medieval terms did not necessarily mean a wooded area, but a wasteland or uncultivated place where special and strict laws were imposed to protect and preserve the King's game - especially deer and wild boar. The imposition of these harsh forest laws provides us with the first written historical reference to a place named Harrogate: in September 1332, someone called 'John of Harrogate' was arraigned before the Forest Court in a case of assault and trespass.

As the royal fashion for hunting wild game in the forest diminished in the later Middle Ages, many local industries, such as farming, mining, weaving and the forging of iron were allowed to take place within its boundaries. The forest provided a stable and well-administered source of employment for the people of hamlets like Bilton-with-Harrogate and Beckwith-with-Rossett, which were later to become the modern Harrogate. Coal and timber from Bilton and Haverah Park helped to power the local forging industry in Nidderdale, and coal was still being taken from Bilton Park as late as the end of the 18th century.

In the early 14th century, the population of the combined hamlets which made up what is now known as Harrogate probably only amounted to about 30 families, perhaps no more than 250 people.

Although the Royal Forest of Knaresborough was owned by the Crown, it was not a crown estate but governed by the Duchy of Lancaster. This had been created by Edward III in 1351. Twenty-one years later, the second Duke of Lancaster, John of Gaunt, gave up the Earldom of Richmond to Richard II, who in return gave the Duke's son, Henry, the Royal Forest of Knaresborough, including what was to be the future Harrogate. But following a quarrel Henry was banished from the country. When his father, John of Gaunt, died, Henry's estates were declared forfeit to Richard II. Henry returned to England to claim his inheritance, carrying all before him and taking the castles of Pickering, Pontefract and Knaresborough in his successful campaign, before defeating Richard II and being crowned Henry IV in 1399.

Henry immediately declared that the Duchy of Lancaster would thereafter be held as a royal possession, thus ensuring Harrogate's royal pedigree of ownership. This was one of the most significant moments in the long history of Harrogate, because it guaranteed that the area of the town would be retained as a royal possession for nearly 380 years, until the Great Enclosure Award of 1778. Even after that, the Duchy continued to own many parts of the town, including, most crucially, the 200 acres of the famous Harrogate Stray.

Following the deprivations of the Harrying of the North and the invasion of the Scots, the Harrogate area had to steel itself to face yet another disaster when the Black Death reached Yorkshire in 1349. No figures have survived of the death rate in the small, largely self-contained communities, but some indication of the affect it had can be seen in the Court Rolls of 1349-50, which record that of the 575 acres which made up Bilton-with-Harrogate,

274 acres were held by tenants who had died in the horrendous outbreak. Perhaps Harrogate recovered better than other places, because unlike in other communities, no land or villages seem to have been abandoned because of deaths from the Black Death, and the clearance of woodland from the ancient forest - known as 'assarting' (see box) - seems to have continued unabated into the 15th century.

A chantry chapel had been set up in 'Harowgate' by 1439, possibly dedicated to St John the Baptist; it had perhaps been endowed by one of the families who leased the hunting in the Knaresborough forest from Queen Philippa, the consort of Edward III, who had been granted the income from the forest in 1331. The regular survey of the forest by inspectors appointed by the Duchy of Lancaster found in 1476 that the park at Bilton was 'gretely hurted and the woods thereof almost destroid by felling of the grete trees' and that 'the pasture of the same park is gretely hurted by wrotyng of swyne.'

Poaching of the king's forest deer was also a real problem during the later 15th century, and a case heard in 1482 accused several men, including the minister of St Robert's Church at Pannal, of the hunting and killing of deer at Harlow and Haverah. Most of the other 15th-century records refer to the various fines imposed and excuses used by local men, some from 'the community of the village of Harowgat', who did not want to become involved in Henry V's endless wars with the French.

Farming was still the most common source of employment and income for the people of the scattered communities which made up present-day Harrogate during the 15th century. Other activities included forestry, weaving and the forging of iron, although the use of timber as a fuel source seems to have died out by the late 14th century. It was replaced by coal and peat extracted from the forest at places like Bilton. Ironstone was also found within the forest boundaries. The name of nearby Kirkby Overblow, a village to the south of Harrogate, means 'the village with a church and smelters'.

Prospecting for ironstone within the forest attracted the attention of the Duchy of Lancaster as a potentially lucrative source of income. It was later said that 'many ironstones were thrown up' and that 'all the ground thereabout being formerly digg'd

> *Did you know?*
> ## Assarting
> *Assarting is the medieval name (deriving from the French 'essarter', meaning 'to remove or grub up woodland') for the winning of new farmland from the waste or forest. Where it took place can often be recognised in elements of surviving place names, such as 'stock', 'stubs' and 'stubbing', which refer to the stumps of felled trees, and 'ridding', 'rudding' and 'royd', which tell of land which has been cleared of trees, particularly in the north of England. Local examples include Rudding Park, Hampsthwaite and Brackenthwaite; 'thwaite' derives from an Old Norse name for a forest clearing.*

up, and all the wood destroyed in Queen Elizabeth's time, by iron-forges'. The Duchy appointed a surveyor, Richard Stanhope, to look into the situation in the Harrogate area in the later 16th century, and it may well have been the search for ironstone which inadvertently was the cause of the discovery of Harrogate's earliest mineral springs.

Of course, we cannot know four centuries on exactly how William Slingsby of Bilton Park came across the first chalybeate spring in the area still known as Bilton-with-Harrogate in 1571, but we do know that the prospecting for ironstone was very intense in the forest at the time. Maybe he was attracted by the flocks of lapwings (locally-known as 'tewits' in imitation of their call) which periodically gathered around the spring to taste the salty crystals which formed from the chalybeate water around its edges (see box). And perhaps it was for that reason he named the spring the Tewit Well.

However it happened, Slingsby's discovery was very fortuitous, because 'taking the waters' had suddenly become very fashionable throughout the country in the late 16th century. New mineral wells were being exploited everywhere in imitation of the already established continental spas, which all took their name from the Belgian town of Spa south-west of Liege in the Hautes Fagnes hills. (The word 'spa' comes from the Walloon word 'espa', meaning 'fountain'.)

Dr Edmund Deane of York's 1626 book 'Spadacrene Anglica - or The English Spaw Fountaine' was the first book to describe the medical benefits of the spa waters of the Harrogate area. Deane refers to Slingsby's discovery of 55 years before 'at Haregate-head', and to its promotion by Dr Timothy Bright, the personal physician to 'Good Queen Bess', Queen Elizabeth I. It is, however, interesting to note that Deane still does not refer to Harrogate by name, but describes on his title page 'the acide, or tart Fountaine in the Foreft of Knaresborow, in the Weft-Riding of Yorkfhire'. It had been Bright in the later years of the 16th century who was the first to name the Harrogate (or Knaresborough) wells as 'the English Spaw' - this, according to Malcolm Neesam, was the first recorded application of the name to an English resort.

Bright actively promoted the health-giving properties of Slingsby's well and Slingsby, quick to realise its potential, swiftly erected a wall around the well-head and had the area around it flagged with stone. Apparently he became a keen drinker of the water himself, showing his customers that he was offering

> ### Did you know?
> #### Lapwings
> *The lapwing (Vanellus vanellus) or tewit, after which Harrogate's first mineral well was named, gets its name from the Old English 'hleapwince', which means 'a leap with a waver in it', which perfectly describes the tumbling mating flight of the black and white wader. It is thought that the birds were attracted to the crystallised salt particles which were left around the edges of the spring.*

them nothing he would not drink himself.

A second chalybeate or iron well, initially known as the Sweet Well and then later as the St John's Well, was discovered in 1631 by Michael Stanhope about half a mile east of the Tewit Well - and the future of High Harrogate as a 'the new English spa' seemed assured.

> ### Did you know?
> #### Harrogate Water
> *The sulphurous waters from the Harrogate wells were a recommended cure for worms and other kinds of internal parasites, which, were said to have affected at least 80 per cent of the population in the 17th century. According to Michael Stanhope, the discoverer of St John's Well, one gentlewoman who journeyed all the way from Sussex to try the waters voided a staggering 100 stones within a fortnight.*

At this time, Harrogate was still just a collection of scattered rural farms and cottages, and there was nowhere for most of the visitors to the wells to stay. So many based themselves in the better-appointed surrounding towns, such as York, Knaresborough, Boroughbridge, Otley and Wetherby. It was only later that the residents of Harrogate realised the income-earning potential of this new rush of visitors, and began to offer simple farmhouse accommodation and food for them. It was from these humble beginnings that Harrogate's great hotel trade began.

The Civil War passed Harrogate by - but only just, as the battle of Marston Moor between the Royalist forces led by Prince Rupert and Lord Leven's successful Parliamentarians took place in 1644 a mere nine miles away. The Royalist forces probably passed through Harrogate on their way to the battle, and soldiers seem to have been billeted there later, causing a few problems, although according to a contemporary account, the Earl of Holland seemed not to like the waters.

It was a sentiment shared by the eminent Essex botanist and naturalist John Ray who was an early visitor to the 'Spaw' after the Restoration. He recorded after his visit in 1661: 'It is not unpleasant to the taste, somewhat acid and vitriolick. Then we visited the sulphur well, whose water, though it be pellucid enough, yet stinks noisomely like rotten eggs or sulphur auratum diaphoreticum'. Lady Verney, who visited the spa in 1665, also obviously felt that the accommodation offered by Harrogate still left much to be desired. She fumed (with little regard to spelling or grammar): '... we arrived att the nasty Spaw, and have now began to drinke the horid sulfer watter, which all thowgh as bad as is posable to be immajened, yet in my judgement plesent, to all the doings we have within doorse, the house and all that is in it being horidly nasty and crowded up with all sorte of company, which we Eate within a roome as the spiders are redy to drope into my mouthe, and sure hathe nethor been well cleaned nor ared this doseuen yerese, it makes me moare sick than the nasty water ...'

The mention of the 'nasty Spaw' and the 'stinking wells' refer to sulphur springs, which had been discovered in Bilton Park, Starbeck, and also in Low Harrogate; the latter was later to become known as the Old Sulphur Well, on the site of the present Royal Pump Room. People were not only drinking these awful-smelling waters, but also bathing in them to cure all kinds of skin complaints.

Celia Fiennes, the daughter of a Civil War general, was equally sniffy about these sulphur springs when, as part of her adventurous side-saddle ride through England in 1697, she visited 'Haragate'. She wrote: '... the Sulpher or Stinking spaw, not improperly term'd for the Smell being so very strong and offensive that I could not force my horse near the Well', and added: '... its a quick purger and very good for all Scurbutick humours; some persons drink a quart or two - I dranke a quart in a morning for two days and hold them to be a good sort of Purge if you can hold your breath so as to drinke them down'.

Others must have been more favourably impressed, however, for in his journal of 1675, Thomas Baskerville describes how he went 'to see the Spa water at Harricate, a village made good by reason of the resort of people to the wells'. But the well-to-do were not the only ones who benefited from the spa's healing waters, and they were always made available to the poor. In 1660, for example, the town constable claimed 7d (3p) for 'carreing one cripple to Harrogait on horseback'.

By this time, the people of Harrogate were realising that they had to improve the accommodation offered to these paying visitors, and the Queen's Head on the road between Harrogate and Knaresborough became the first hotel to open in the late 17th century. It was soon followed by others in High Harrogate, such as the Granby (originally known as the Sinking Ship), the Dragon and the Salutation, and in Low Harrogate, the Crown was established near the 'stinking' Old Sulphur Well. The scene was set for the Georgian heyday of what was to become England's greatest spa.

The 'Stinking Spaw'

The Royal Pump Room in Crown Place was still known as the Sulphur Well when this photograph was taken. It stands on the site of the 'Stinking Spaw' which was so offensive to early visitors such as Lady Verney and Celia Fiennes, and still claims to have the world's strongest known sulphur spring. The present octagonal, domed building was designed in the classical style by Isaac Thomas Shutt, son of the licensee of the Swan Inn who discovered the controversial Thackway Well in 1835. It took the place of an old stone temple dating from 1808, which was removed and re-erected over the original Tewit Well. An annexe was later added in 1913, but since 1953, the building has been a museum telling the story of Harrogate spa.

SULPHUR WELL 1897 39426

SPAWING AT HARROGATE.
BEFORE taking the Waters!

SPAWING ZZZ02029

SPAWING AT HARROGATE.

She: "Pardon me! but do they drink it cold or hot?"
He: "It don't matter which way, mum, as it always touches the spot."

SPAWING ZZZ02027

SPAWING AT HARROGATE.
Serving the Waters.

Flavouring the Waters.
Old Satan, he knows, and knows it full well,
What does for his customers where he does dwell
So the overflow sulphur he pumps up on high
To cure poor devils who don' care to die.

SPAWING ZZZ02028

Early History 19

THE ROYAL PUMP ROOM, 1902 48974

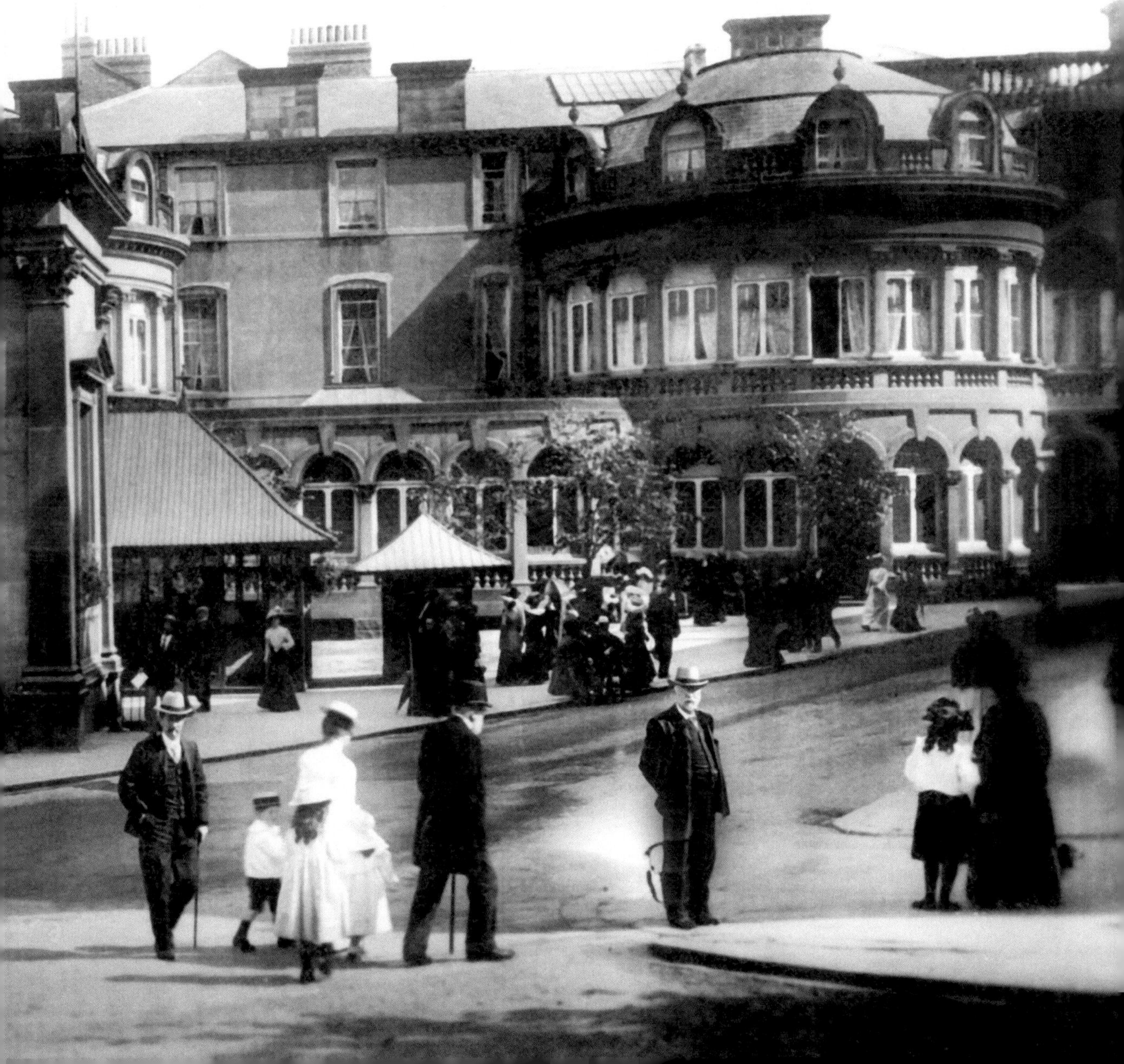

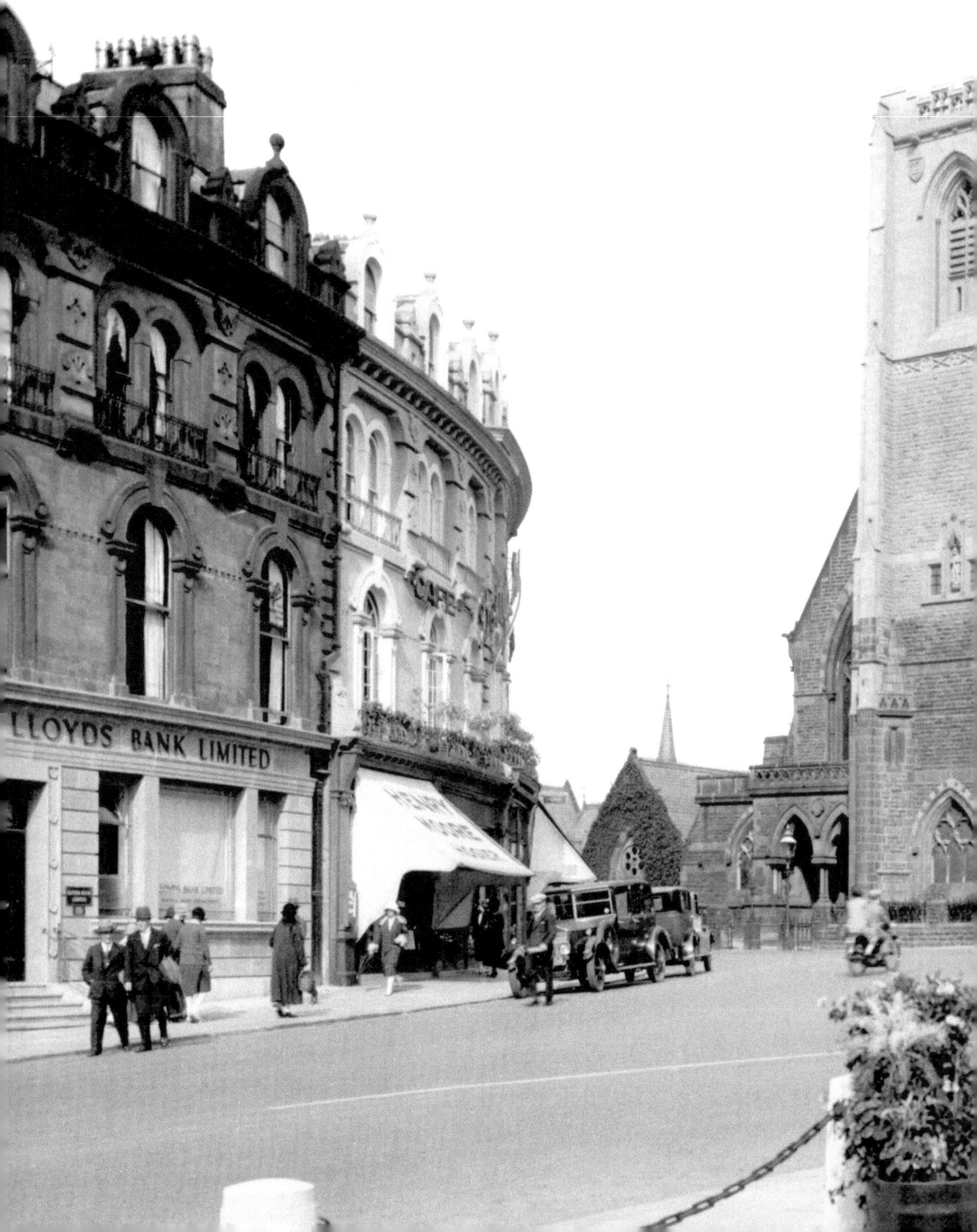
LLOYDS BANK LIMITED

CHAPTER TWO

The Spa Years

THE GREAT ENCLOSURE Award of 1778 ranks alongside the 1399 claiming of the Forest of Knaresborough as part of the Duchy of Lancaster in terms of its importance in securing Harrogate's unique history of accessible public land. England at the time was at the height of the Enclosure Movement. This was a government-enforced measure designed to speed up the gradual enclosure of what was formerly the open field system of farming, which had existed since the Middle Ages and had given every villager the right to use common land and parts of the open field in rotation. The aim was to speed up agricultural reform and make food production more efficient, but there was much local opposition to what today would probably be called the privatisation of the land. The main benefactors were undoubtedly the larger landowners, who could afford to enclose with hedging and walling, whereas the smaller landowners and landless poor had their ancient rights of use of common land summarily taken away from them.

Wherever leading landowners wanted the enclosure of commons and common fields, they would petition Parliament to pass the necessary act to allow this to happen. Then commissioners, usually fellow landowners, would assess the land in question, and a surveyor and valuer would be appointed to award and allocate the new ownerships, theoretically on the basis of what had been held there before. It has been estimated that from 1700 there were about 5,400 of these Enclosure Acts, affecting about seven million acres (2.8 million hectares) of common land and common fields in England. It was probably the most important single factor in the shaping of our modern, patchwork-quilt countryside.

The first step towards the Enclosure Act affecting the Royal Forest of Knaresborough took place in July 1767, when George II issued a commission to formalise the boundaries of the forest. From the start, the appointed commissioners made special reference to the 'medicinal nature' of the mineral springs at Harrogate which were, in their words, 'resorted to by a great number of persons of all ranks'.

When the first act authorising the enclosure of the 20,000 acres of the forest was passed by Parliament in 1770, it too recognised the special nature of the 200 acres of common land now known as the Stray (meaning 'land grazed, or strayed over, by cattle') in the centre of Harrogate. The act unequivocally stated: 'The said two hundred acres of land shall, for ever, hereafter, remain open and unenclosed; and all persons whomsoever shall and may have free access at all times to the said springs, and be at liberty to use and drink the waters there arising, and take the benefit thereof, and shall and may have, use, and enjoy full and free ingress, egress and regress, in, upon, and over, the said two hundred acres of land and any part thereof, without being subject to the payment of any acknowledgement whatsoever for the same, or liable to any action of trespass, or other suit, molestation, or disturbance whatsoever, in respect thereof'.

When the final version of the Award was set down in August 1778, it made several special provisions which were designed to protect the integrity of the Stray and the mineral wells for which the town was already quite famous. The wells were not to be enclosed, so the right of free public access to them was guaranteed, since the land around them was to remain open. This would allow those people who had taken advantage of the medicinal waters the capacity to exercise freely and enjoy the fresh air. It also ensured that the area of the Stray, which was still in the ownership of the Duchy of Lancaster, would not be built on in future years, providing Harrogate with its unique green heart.

The importance of the Great Award of 1778 to the future character of Harrogate is difficult to underestimate, because it gave the town its essential shape which has survived to this day. It also set the scene for Harrogate's extraordinary growth as England's top spa during its Georgian heyday.

Under the 1778 Award, the Stray had been divided into 50 so-called 'gates' consisting of four acres each, where 'stinted' grazing rights for a specified number of beasts were available for purchase. A single gate owner was able to keep a cow of more than two years old; two calves; or four sheep, including ewes with unweaned lambs. A three-year-old horse was said to require one and a half gates. The thinking was that under this strictly regulated system of grazing, and with the Duchy retaining ownership, the Stray would be kept in good condition for the townspeople and visitors to the spa.

A further act affecting the Stray was passed by Parliament in 1798 granting the town a further 15 acres of land on the Stray along the Otley, Hookstone and Wetherby roads. This was to compensate gate owners for the loss of grazing caused by new road and footpath building. The enclosure commissioners were

THE STRAY 1888 20922

This view of the Stray gives a good idea of how important the unique green open space at the heart of Harrogate is to the town. In the background are the Prospect Hotel and Prospect Crescent.

also given the power to make new rules for the administration of the Stray.

Visitors were still flocking to the town. Among the most distinguished in around 1725 was the author and journalist Daniel Defoe, author of 'Robinson Crusoe', during a journey round Britain; his account of this journey, 'A Tour through the Whole Island of Great Britain', was published between 1724-27. Defoe was usually rather cynical about what he called 'country wonders', and had been particularly scathing about the so-called Wonders of the Peak. But when he came to what was still being called the 'Knaresborough Spaw', he described the 'Sweet Spaw' (the Tewit Well) and the 'Stinking Spaw' (the Sulphur Well) as 'valuable rarities, and not to be equalled in England'. He was surprised in so remote a place to find a great many of what he termed 'good company' drinking the waters, more than he was to find later in Scarborough. This was in spite of the fact that 'this seems to be a most desolate out-of-the-world place, and that men would only retire to it for religious mortifications, and to hate the world, but we found it quite otherwise'.

All physicians acknowledged the 'vitriolic water' of the Sweet Spa, said Defoe, to be 'a very sovereign medicine in several particular distempers', while his description of the Sulphur Spa echoed that of Lady Verney and Celia Fiennes: 'This water is clear as crystal, but fetid and nauseous to the smell, so that those who drink it are obliged to hold their noses when they drink; yet it is a valuable medicine also in scorbutic, hypochondriac, and especially in hydropic distempers'. He added with typical cynicism: '... as to its curing the gout, I take that, as in other cases, ad referendum'.

The first illustrations of the Harrogate wells started to appear at about this time in the earliest guidebooks, and Moses Griffith's coloured engraving of 1772, held in Harrogate Museum, still shows a predominantly rural scene. Against a background of trees and isolated stone cottages, people are arriving on horseback or in horse-drawn cabs to the stone-

ADVERTISEMENT ZZZ02031

The Spa Years

> ### Did you know?
> #### The Origin of the Waters
> *One of the most popular theories during the 18th century to explain Harrogate's famous mineral springs was that they were the result of timbers sunk deep underground, which had gradually rotted away beneath a bed of earth and moss. This was long before more scientific explanations proved that they were the result of magmatic or plutonic waters rising from deep within the earth's crust.*

built structures which shelter the Sulphur Wells in Low Harrogate. The men are dressed in breeches and wearing cocked, tricorn hats, while the ladies are wearing long dresses as they stand around obviously deep in conversation. The social aspects of being seen to be 'taking the waters' were obviously becoming just as important as the actual cure.

Famous Patients

Many famous people travelled to Harrogate to take the waters in its Georgian heyday. Among them were General Robert Clive of India, who stayed at the Granby in 1763, (when apparently he would work on important state papers on a table placed in the window of the Long Room); Prime Minister Lord Bute, who visited in the same year; the novelist Tobias Smollett in 1766 (who later described his experiences in his novel 'Humphry; the Lord Chancellor, Alexander Wedderburn, later the first Earl of Rosslyn (who later built Wedderburn House, where he would stay on his journeys north in 1786); the statesman Lord Castlereagh in 1801; the poet Lord Byron, who stayed at the Crown in 1806; and the Lake District Romantic poets, William Wordsworth and Robert Southey, who visited with their families in 1827.

THE CROWN HOTEL 1902 48972

One factor, however, seems to have made Harrogate stand apart from other, perhaps more fashionable, spas of the Georgian era, such as Bath: there seems always to have been a more democratic and less formal air about the process of taking the waters here, perhaps as a result of the genuine friendliness of the local Yorkshire people. George Carey, describing his visit in 1796, wrote: 'There is little etiquette at Harrowgate, nor are the company pestered with the officious and interested cringings of an obsequious Master of Ceremonies'. At this time, most of the other spas in Britain, such as Bath, Cheltenham, Leamington and Scarborough, appointed a Master of Ceremonies, usually a man of high standing, whose job it was to 'educate' the visiting public in matters of polite behaviour and decorum. Harrogate, to its credit, resolutely refused to dictate to its visitors in that overbearing manner, and democratically allowed each hotel to elect its own Master of Ceremonies from among its guests, which usually resulted in the longest-staying guest gaining the post, whatever his standing in society.

By this time, other facilities beside the wells and new hotels were being added every year to the attractions of Harrogate. Low Harrogate's Old Sulphur Well - 'the Stinking Spaw' - was just as popular as High Harrogate's St John's Well, so plans were prepared by Thomas Chippendale for an octagonal, open-sided temple-like building to be erected over the well. The £230 building was paid for by public subscription and completed in 1808. It was removed to the Tewit Well in 1842.

The first theatre was built in the town as early as 1788, replacing the barn which had been used for that purpose at the front of the Granby Hotel in High Harrogate. It remains one of Harrogate's finest Georgian buildings, now a private dwelling known as Mansfield House. Samuel Butler's north country touring ensemble were regular performers during the high season, and ticket prices for the unreserved seats ranged from 3s (15p) for a box seat and 1s (5p) in the gallery. Performances took place on Tuesdays, Thursdays and Saturdays, and the choice of what was staged was often left to the elected MC who was currently staying at the local hostelry.

Did you know?

Thomas Chippendale

Thomas Chippendale of Otley, the famous English cabinetmaker who gave his name to a style of furniture which is still being made today, designed the Tuscan-columned, domed Roman temple which first enclosed the Old Sulphur Well in Low Harrogate in 1808. The building, on the site of the Royal Pump Room, was paid for by public subscription and completed in 1808.

The Spa Years

The Crown is one of Harrogate's oldest hotels; among its guests was Lord Byron in 1806.

THE CROWN HOTEL 1902 48973

THE CROWN HOTEL 2004 ZZZ02007 (John Morrison)

30 HARROGATE – *a history and celebration of the town*

THE CROWN HOTEL 1902 48972

The Spa Years 31

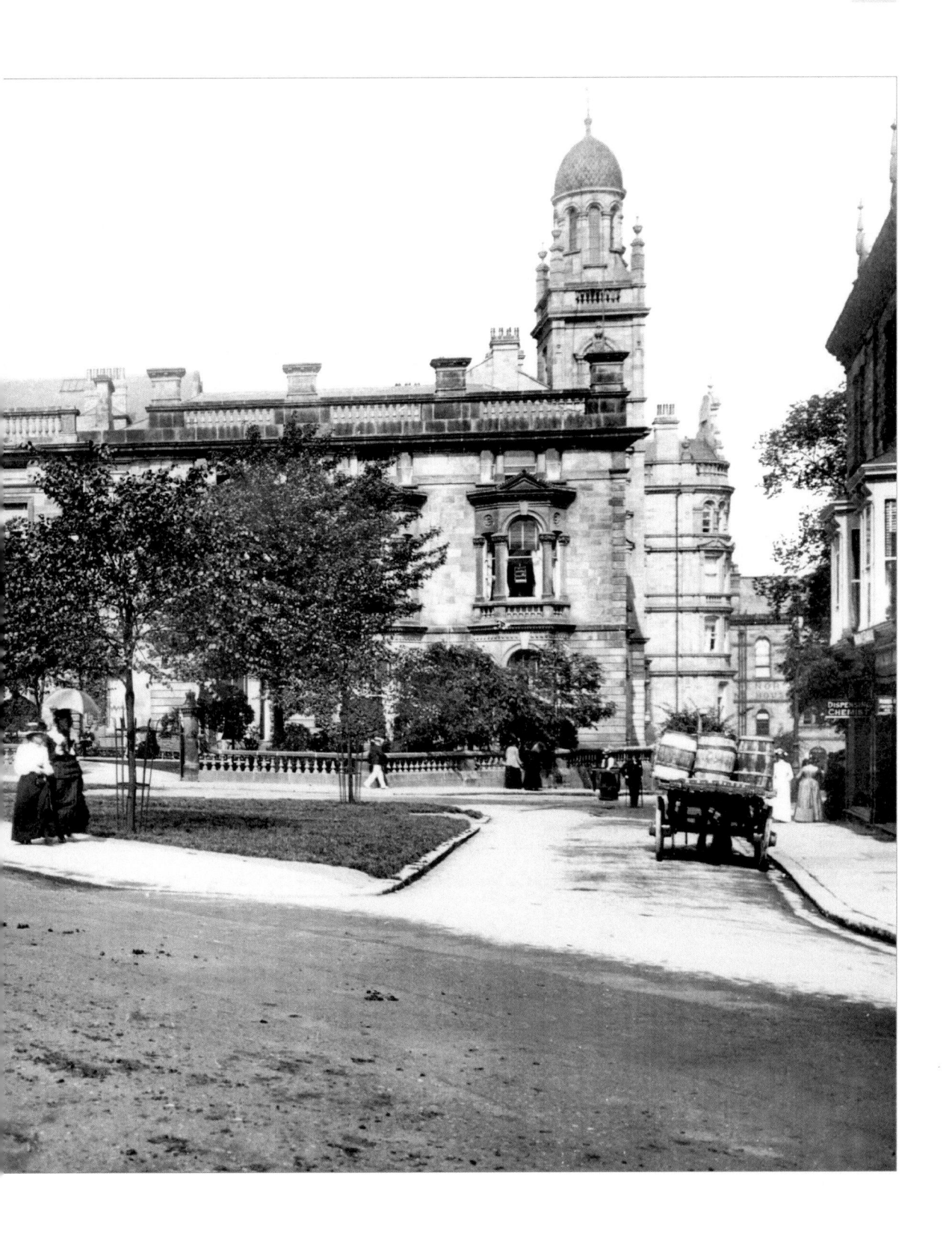

32 HARROGATE – *a history and celebration of the town*

ST MARY'S CHURCH 1891 28311

The Spa Years

Balls were also held regularly in turn at hotels such as the Dragon, the Crown and the Granby, to which guests staying at the other hotels were invited. Concerts featuring the work of contemporary composers such as Handel and Haydn were also staged.

The cultural well-being of visitors was catered for not only by the theatre but also by a subscription library, which was opened by local bookseller Eli Hargrove in High Harrogate around 1775. There were also billiard rooms, archery butts and a racecourse, which had been constructed in 1793, on the Stray. Harrogate was, in its elegant Georgian heyday, a visitor attraction to rival the modern day Blackpool or Brighton.

By 1801, the permanent population of the burgeoning town was 1,600 souls, and this was to reach 2,000 a decade later as the reputation of the efficacy of taking the evil-smelling sulphurous waters spread throughout the country.

It was long before the advent of proper local government, and the town at this time was still being run by what were known as vestry or town meetings, held by rotation in various hotels. These meetings, attended by civic-minded local business people, innkeepers and doctors, started to provide other facilities for the town, including a grand promenade or assembly room which opened in 1806 on Swan Road, Lower Harrogate, in what is now the Mercer Art Galley. Here, visitors could relax or attend recitals, dances and lectures in pleasant surroundings out of

Did you know?
Vandalism

Vandalism is not just a modern problem. In 1821-22, the townspeople of Harrogate complained to the Duchy of Lancaster that 'during the night time, some persons unknown to your petitioners have put into the said Mineral Springs, quantities of Dung, Ashes, Dead Dogs and other animals of a most offensive nature'. As if the smell of the sulphur was not bad enough!

Blind Jack of Knaresborough

One of the great characters of 18th-century Harrogate was Jack Metcalf, better known as Blind Jack of Knaresborough, the famous sightless Yorkshire road maker; he was responsible for many of the turnpike roads constructed in the district, including the Boroughbridge turnpike and the road between Harrogate and Harewood Bridge. Jack hailed from nearby Knaresborough, and had been blinded by smallpox at the age of six. He served as an engineer and bandsman under General Wade in Scotland, where he learnt the skills of road building, and he constructed about 200 miles (320km) of roads in the north of England. He was invited to Harrogate to be the resident fiddler at the Queen's Head Hotel in 1732, and became a popular local celebrity at local inns and hotels. A big man (he weighed 17 stone) of many talents, he arranged the town's first transport hire service, and later scandalously eloped with the daughter of the Granby Hotel's landlord on the eve of her wedding.

the sometimes adverse Yorkshire weather. A fine new workhouse was built at Starbeck in 1810; it took not only the homeless and destitute of Harrogate, but also those of surrounding towns and villages.

Civic concern for the less favoured and poorer members of society is a recurring theme in Harrogate's history. As early as 1775, subscriptions were being raised in local hostelries for the benefit of the poor taking the waters, no doubt partly owing to the problems they were causing by congregating around the wells in large numbers. Whether the motives were purely altruistic or not, a committee was set up in 1818 with the intention of opening a new subscription for the erection of baths which would be solely for the use of the poor. The new Bath Hospital, eventually to become the Royal Bath Hospital in Valley Gardens, opened for its first patients in 1826 - with a set of strict rules barring its patients from loitering around the wells and parks frequented by visitors.

The spiritual welfare of the townspeople was not overlooked either, and, in 1831, the dilapidated chapel of St John, which had been built in 1749 on Duchy of Lancaster land, was finally replaced by the Early English-style Christ Church in a triangular isolated island on the Stray. The stone from the older building was re-used by the Congregationalist church to build their new Providence chapel on the corner of John Street and James Street.

The first St Mary's Church in Low Harrogate was built between 1824-25, again on land donated by the Duchy, at the instigation of Joseph Thackwray, the entrepreneurial owner of the Crown Hotel. The designer was Samuel Chapman, the architect of the Royal Bath Hospital. The present rather plain-looking St Mary's was built in 1916 to replace the older church, which had to be closed after it had been declared unsafe in 1904.

CHRIST CHURCH 1938 88346

ST MARY'S CHURCH, LOW HARROGATE 1862 ZZZ02030

St Mary's Church

The original St Mary's Church had been built in 1824-25 to provide Low Harrogate with a place of worship to match High Harrogate's Chapel of St John. It resulted from a successful public petition to the Duchy of Lancaster for a church to serve the people of Low Harrogate in 1821, and was erected following the raising of various subscriptions among the great and the good. The Early English-style design was by Samuel Chapman, the architect of the Royal Bath Hospital, and the total cost was £3,137 - the most expensive church ever built in Harrogate at the time. Chapman's St Mary's did not last long: it was closed in 1904 as being unsafe, and the church was rebuilt in 1916.

ST MARY'S CHURCH 1891 28311x

Work on St Peter's Church, in the centre of town, began in 1871 and was completed five years later. The imposing Perpendicular-style tower, which so dominates Prospect Place, was not added to the Victorian church until the 1920s.

The Wesleyan Methodists had erected their first meeting-house on Park Parade as early as 1796, but the town's major Methodist chapel was not built until 1824 by James Simpson. The Victoria Avenue Congregational Church, which is such a prominent feature in views from the Stray, was built in 1862 on West Park Stray.

The Ionic-style Victoria Baths, the first public baths in Harrogate, were built at the instigation of local businessman John Williams in 1833. Not to be outdone, a year later Joseph Thackwray opened his Tuscan-style Montpellier Baths in the grounds of his Crown Hotel. While digging the foundations of his new baths, Thackwray discovered no fewer than six new wells, including four valuable new sulphur wells.

Meanwhile, Williams was busy constructing the magnificent Royal Promenade and Cheltenham Spa Rooms, near the recently-discovered Cheltenham Well, named after the Gloucestershire spa, on the corner of what later was to become King's Road and Ripon Road. The building opened with a grand ball in August 1835, and the classic Doric columns of its entrance and its opulent, barrel-roofed interior rivalled anything which could be

ST PETER'S CHURCH 1927 80225

found elsewhere in an English spa. It really put Harrogate on the map.

The rivalry between these leading local entrepreneurs came to a head in 1835, when, shortly after the opening of Williams's Spa Rooms, it was discovered that the Old Sulphur Well - Harrogate's principal claim to fame and the basis of its economy - was draining away. When the situation was investigated, it was found that Joseph Thackwray had ordered the digging of a well in a nearby shop, apparently to deliberately divert the waters from the public sulphur well to his private estate. The balloon went up immediately, and Thackwray was served with a notice to stop the work or face prosecution. It is significant that the notice was signed by his major rival, John Williams of the Victoria Baths, along with several other hotel owners.

Arguments raged back and forth for two years as various tests were taken at the wells concerned, and eventually the case of the 'Thackwray well' was heard at York Assizes in March 1837. The basis of the prosecution case against Thackwray was the clause in the 1770 Enclosure Act which protected the wells on the Stray for the use of the public, and which prohibited the sinking of any workings which might damage or affect them. The judge, Baron Alderson, eventually got both parties to agree to the compromise that in exchange for the dropping of the case against him, Thackwray would make the new well and shop over for public use, and agree not to deepen any other of his wells.

However, the case made it obvious that the old legislation was not adequate to protect Harrogate's major asset, and in 1840, Samuel Powell, a respected local solicitor, steward of the Royal Forest and agent for the Duchy of Lancaster (who had acted both for Thackwray and his opponents during the 1837 case), advised his masters of the urgent need for new legislation. The result was the Harrogate Improvement Act of 1841 which, at the instigation of the Duchy, not only gave better protection to the mineral wells and the Stray, but also granted powers to provide a market for the town, to light its streets, to appoint constables, to purchase or rent buildings, and to construct new roads and footpaths, sewers and drains. Twenty-one commissioners were elected by the residents of High and Low Harrogate at the end of May 1841 to implement the provisions of the new act.

By the time the young Queen Victoria ascended to the throne in 1837, the population of Harrogate had risen to just over 4,000, yet it was still managing to retain that rural character which so endeared itself to visitors. Dr Granville, author of an authoritative survey of British spas in 1841, noted: 'Harrogate has the elements of becoming a Spa of the first magnitude, even to the extent of attracting foreign travellers ... It is not one of your ephemeral Spas, dependent on fashion ... it remains a village. Those (the waters) of Harrogate are unsophisticated because the place itself remains as it was.'

But could Harrogate retain that unspoiled and unaffected natural environment in the face of increasing urbanisation during the Victorian era?

The Spa Years

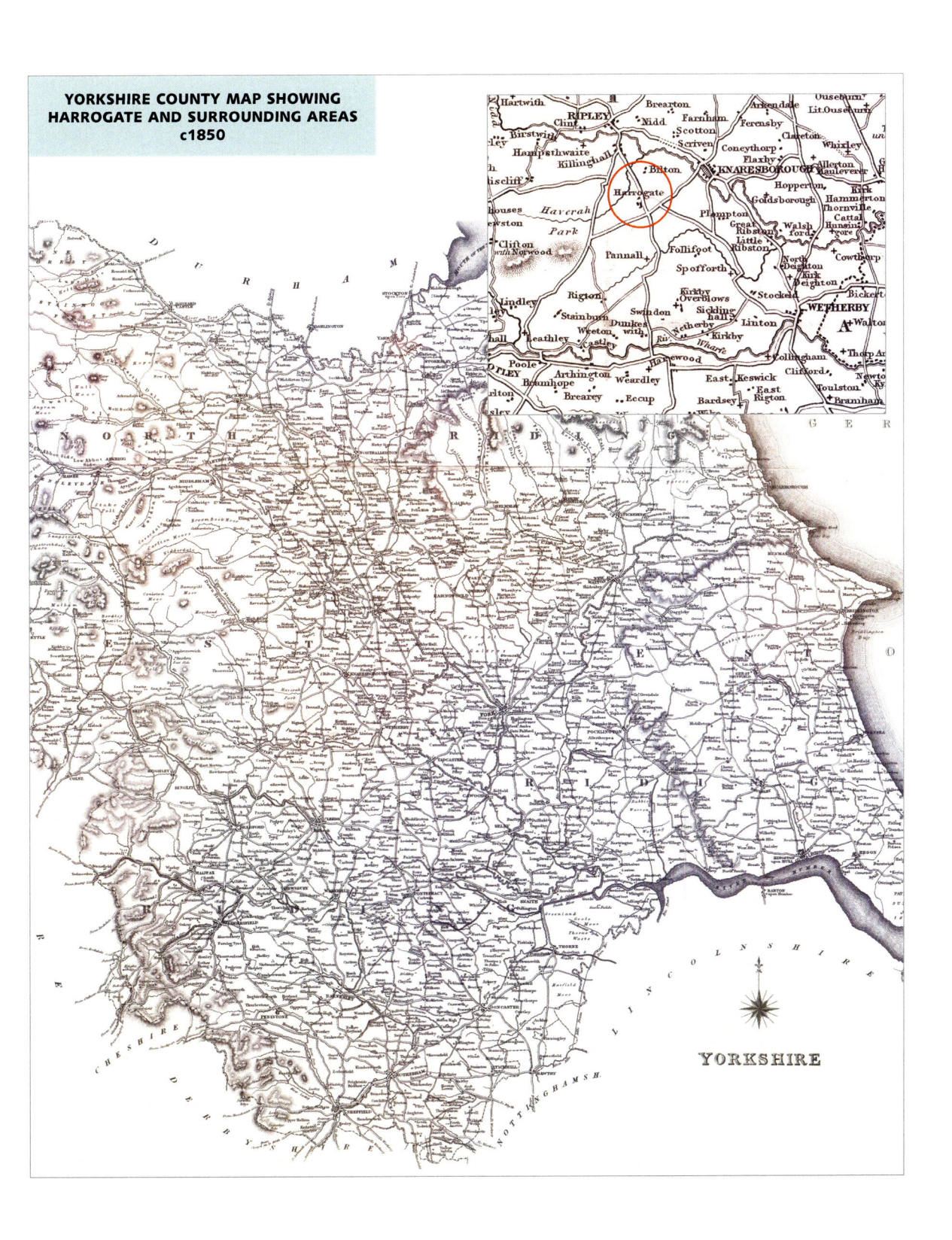

YORKSHIRE COUNTY MAP SHOWING HARROGATE AND SURROUNDING AREAS c1850

HOTE
THE CAFÉ.
EDWARD STANDING. LIMITED.
GROCERY AND PROVIS
TEA & COFFEE SALES
E. STANDING Ld
HOT JOINTS FROM 12 TO 3
HOTEL RESTAURANT
ATION HOTEL
GENTLEMENS HAIR DRESSING SALOONS

CHAPTER THREE

Victorian Harrogate

LOW HARROGATE 1853 ZZZ02016

THE STATUE of a sombre-faced Queen Victoria, standing inside her slender Gothic spired monument in Station Square, Harrogate, has seen many changes since it was unveiled with great ceremony by the Marquis of Ripon on 6 October 1887.

The monument had been given to the town on land in James Street donated by Alderman Richard Ellis, a prominent Improvement Commissioner and one of Victorian Harrogate's greatest benefactors. The foundation stone for the monument was laid by the alderman's wife on 14 April, and the Gothic canopy within which the statue stands was designed by a local architect named Bown. The statue itself was by the London sculptor Webber. The structure was originally surrounded by decorative cast iron railings and gas lamps, but these were removed during the Second World War munitions crisis, and the monument now stands in a flower bed.

The reason for the grand construction was the Queen's Golden Jubilee, and this was just one of several events in the town by which her loyal townspeople marked the 50th anniversary of her reign. The millionaire inventor and notable benefactor Samson Fox, shortly to become Harrogate's mayor, provided an ox-roasting for the people of the town, which was held on the Stray in glorious sunshine - described at the time as 'Queen's weather' - on June 20. The spit holding the huge ox carcass turned for a whole day, as a band played to entertain the people coming along for the free feast. As they danced their way across the grassy sward, Fox had arranged displays of the new electric lighting to illuminate the scene. Free bread and beer were provided when on

VICTORIA MONUMENT, STATION SQUARE 2004
ZZZ02006 (John Morrison)

Queen Victoria still gazes out over Station Square today.

Station Square

This view shows the Victoria Monument in Station Square, with passengers queuing beneath it to board a charabanc, perhaps for a trip to Fountains Abbey or Plumpton Rocks, popular excursions from Harrogate at the time. The Station Hotel is in the background and an apron-clad tradesman - perhaps a baker - takes his goods in a basket across town on the right.

STATION SQUARE 1911 63520p

the next day the great carcass was carved. Although the Victorians are today generally regarded as fairly straight-laced, they certainly knew how to enjoy themselves; however the records show that the police inspector and the two constables who were on duty for the celebrations were not called into action.

In many ways, the celebration of Queen Victoria's jubilee marked the high point of life in Victorian Harrogate. The Victorian age was a period of tremendous growth and prosperity for the spa town, and this was largely due to the far-sighted enthusiasm and civic spirit of businessmen like Richard Ellis, the son of a Harrogate blacksmith. He had served his apprenticeship as a cabinetmaker before going on to enjoy a very successful career as a builder, but he was a man who always put the interests of the town first.

The local historian Malcolm Neesam has dubbed Richard Ellis 'the Father of Victorian Harrogate', and there is no doubting the considerable influence he had on the development of the town during that exciting period of growth. He was a distinguished mayor of the town from 1884-87, and had been elected to the board of the Improvement Commissioners in 1855.

Principal among the many notable civic achievements which Ellis oversaw was the Commissioners' new Victoria Baths in what was later to become Crescent Gardens. Ellis himself laid the foundation stone in 1871 for this splendid new public building with its imposing entrance hall and ticket office, with offices for the Improvement Commissioners above. The baths itself included individual baths for men and women and two immersion pools, and soon eclipsed the other public baths in the town in popularity.

Victoria Baths

This view of the Victoria Baths was taken 17 years after its opening from a deserted street in what was later to become Crescent Gardens. Alderman Richard Ellis was the guiding spirit behind the new building. He laid the foundation stone of this stylish new public facility, which also housed the offices of the Improvement Commissioners above the entrance hall (centre left), in February, 1871. The E-shaped building with its two-storey central block included individual facilities for men and women and two immersion pools. The Victoria Baths were later replaced when they were converted to become the offices of the borough council after major alterations in 1930.

VICTORIA BATHS 1888 20940

Victorian Harrogate

THE COUNCIL OFFICES 2004 ZZZ02000 (John Morrison)

The former Victoria Baths now serve as offices for the council.

THE CENTRAL PHARMACY ZZZ02011

Wilson the chemist became Mayor of Harrogate 1896/97.

Ellis (along with other people, including Queen Victoria and Sampson Fox) also made the endowment which made the town's first hospital, later the Royal Bath Hospital, possible; he constructed the new Methodist Ashville School (1877) and the Victoria Park Methodist Church, and successfully led the campaign which eventually provided the town with its first fire engine.

Ellis never saw the results of his last great idea - a great bathing and hydrotherapy centre to rival those at Bath and Matlock - come to fruition in the shape of the Royal Baths, to be built on the site of the old Montpellier Baths. But by the time of his death in 1895, the site had already been acquired; the Royal Baths were opened in time to mark the old Queen's Diamond Jubilee in 1897.

Meanwhile, a number of commercial hydropathic establishments were being set up; for example, the Cairn Hydro in Ripon Road was opened in 1889, and boasted its own Turkish baths, tennis courts and spacious gardens. It suffered a disastrous fire in 1891, but recovered to become one of Harrogate's smartest hotels.

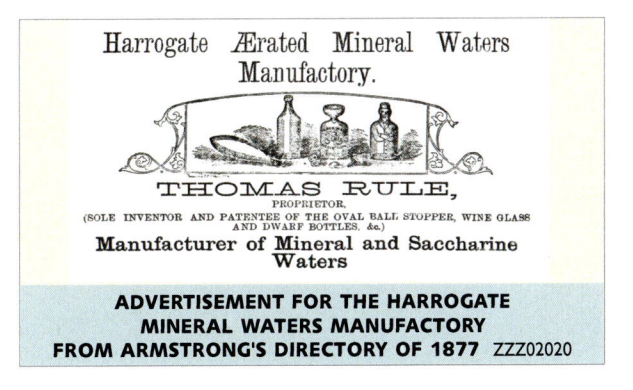

ADVERTISEMENT FOR THE HARROGATE MINERAL WATERS MANUFACTORY FROM ARMSTRONG'S DIRECTORY OF 1877 ZZZ02020

HARROGATE – *a history and celebration of the town*

THE ROYAL BATH HOSPITAL 1892 30627

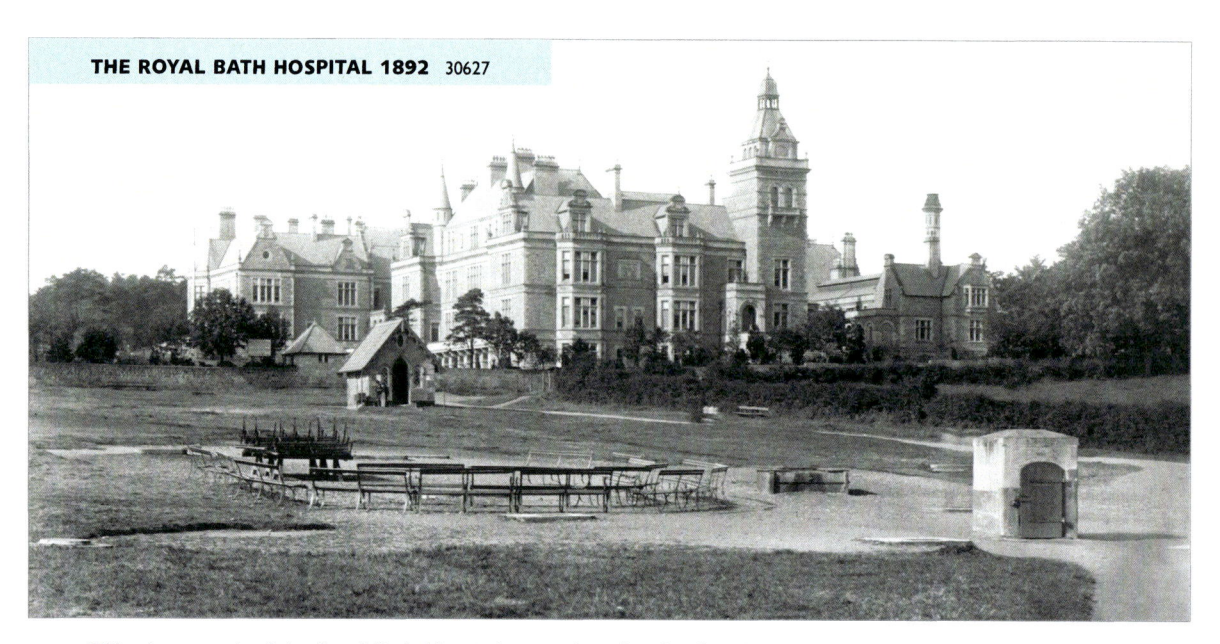

This photograph of the Royal Bath Hospital was taken shortly after the major rebuilding which took place in 1889. It closed in 1994, and is now in residential use.

HARROGATE LADIES' COLLEGE 1927 80228

Harrogate Ladies' College was founded by G M Savery in 1893, and moved to its present site in Clarence Drive some years later. Its chapel was constructed from the demolished remains of St Mary's Church and opened in 1923.

Victorian Harrogate 47

THE CAIRN HYDRO 1902 48985

This shows the front drive and exterior of the Cairn Hydro - now the Cairn Hotel.

THE WINTER GARDENS, THE CAIRN HYDRO c1940 H26006

Wicker chairs grace the Winter Gardens (or conservatory) of the Cairn Hotel.

Another key Victorian benefactor was George Dawson, another master builder who developed from humble beginnings as an apprentice cooper to become one of the most respected developers of high-class villas in Harrogate. The quality of Dawson's building work was largely due to his use of the Bristol-based architect J H Hirst, universally known as 'Hirst of Bristol'. Elected as an Improvement Commissioner in 1870, Dawson died shortly before he was to be elevated to the post of mayor in 1889.

John Barber, landlord of the George Hotel, was another of Harrogate's 'movers and shakers' during the Victorian period. Elected an Improvement Commissioner in 1849, he was the driving force behind the long-drawn-out battle to give Harrogate its own public market; this was something which the Commissioners had been empowered to do from their inception, but it had been delayed by endless arguments which extended over the best part of a quarter of a century. It was largely as a result of Barber's persistence and enthusiasm for the scheme that finally, on 28 February 1874, amid scenes of great pomp and ceremony, he laid the foundation stone for the new market building, which had been designed by Arthur Hiscoe. Barber perceptively remarked at the dinner which followed the opening of the market hall in August, 1874: 'Harrogate has made its way in spite of its inhabitants.'

One of the first tasks that Richard Ellis and his fellow Commissioners had faced was to improve and enhance the future of the town's greatest asset, the Old Sulphur Well, which had been threatened in the notorious Thackwray case. After holding a public competition, they announced that the new Royal Pump Room would be designed by Isaac Shutt, son of the landlord of the Swan Inn, who incidentally had been the person who had first discovered the leaking well six years before.

Shutt's classical octagonal domed building, constructed in local stone at a cost of £3,000, was to become the symbol and icon of the town to the present day. The old stone temple of 1808 was dismantled and re-erected over the site of the original Tewit Well, and Shutt at the same time designed another octagonal pump room at St John's Well. The new Royal Pump Room opened as the centrepiece of the smart Crown Place on 21 July 1842. Later, a temporary annexe was attached to the building; it was not replaced with a permanent domed annexe until 1913, when it was opened by no less than the Lord Mayor of London.

GEORGE HOTEL LETTERHEAD 1899 ZZZ02026

Victorian Harrogate 49

Horse-drawn traps wait outside the George Hotel, owned by John Barber, the man behind Harrogate's first public market.

THE GEORGE HOTEL 1902 48982

THE ROYAL PUMP ROOM INTERIOR 1852 ZZZ02014

THE ROYAL PUMP ROOM 2004
ZZZ02008 (John Morrison)

The Royal Pump Room as it looks today.

What's in the Waters?

An analysis of the waters of Harrogate's Old Sulphur Well by Professor Hofmann published in 'Black's Guide to the County of York' in 1886 revealed that a gallon contained:

Solid contents (grams)		Gaseous contents (cubic inches)	
Sulphate of lime	0.182	Carbonic acid	22.02
Carbonate of lime	12.365	Carbonated hydrogen	5.84
Chloride of calcium	81.735	Sulphurated hydrogen	5.31
Chloride of magnesium	55.693	Nitrogen	2.91
Chloride of potassium	64.701		
Chloride of sodium	866.180		
Sulphide of sodium	15.479		
Silica	0.246		

Did you know?
Harrogate's Springs

One of the strangest things about Harrogate's famous mineral wells is that of the scores of springs which reach the surface, no two are exactly identical in their chemical analysis. This extraordinary variety prompted the author of 'Thorpe's Illustrated Guide to Harrogate', published in 1886, to boast: '... within an area of two or three miles, Harrogate possesses (with slight analytical variations) springs analogous to all the mineral waters spread over the whole of Europe, except hot and seltzer springs'. In Bog Field, Valley Gardens, an astonishing total of 36 different mineral springs come to the surface, prompting it to be hailed as 'a wonder of the natural world'. That did not stop the council from destroying the historic well heads in the 1970s.

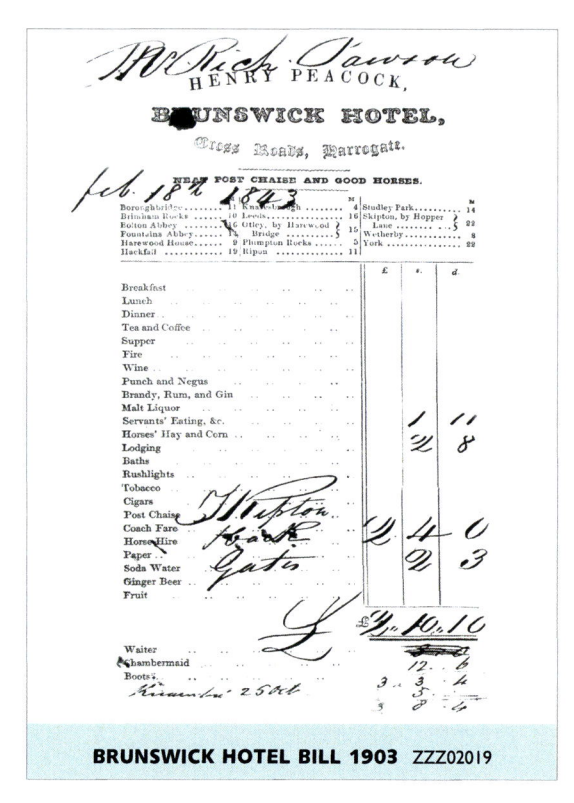

BRUNSWICK HOTEL BILL 1903 ZZZ02019

The Brunswick Hotel is now the Prince of Wales Mansions.

Within twenty years, the number of visitors who came to drink the waters at the Royal Pump Room had risen to nearly 7,000 annually and by 1863 the number had risen to nearly 11,000, boosted considerably at this time by the long overdue coming of the railway to the town. Before then, visitors arrived by stagecoach, and the town's four coaching inns could accommodate up to 30 carriages with stabling for 100 horses. In 1838, there were 18 daily departures by stagecoaches named the Rocket, the Dart, the True Briton, the Tally-ho and the Teazle from Harrogate to places as far away as Newcastle and Manchester, York, Leeds and Selby.

At about the same time as the opening of the Pump Room, the Leeds & Thirsk Railway Company had begun to survey a route from Leeds to Harrogate, Ripon and Thirsk. It involved the building of a low viaduct across the valley of the Crimple Beck from Pannal, and approached Harrogate at Starbeck, where the line was to terminate. A bill was passed by Parliament for the new railway in July 1844.

At the same time, the York & North Midland Railway Company was considering making a connection to the burgeoning and potentially lucrative spa at Harrogate from their line. It would run from the main line at Church Fenton, via Tadcaster, Thorpe Arch, Deighton and Spofforth, reaching the outskirts of Harrogate via the Prospect Tunnel and another huge viaduct across the Crimple Valley, entering central Harrogate by another tunnel under Langcliffe Avenue. The York & North Midland branch line received Parliamentary approval in July 1845.

It is perhaps hard to understand the attitude today, but at the time there was considerable opposition among innkeepers and hoteliers to the coming of the railway to Harrogate. They feared that the town would be flooded with a lower class of visitor from the new industrial towns of Leeds and Bradford, the same sentiment employed by William Wordsworth to oppose the coming of the railway to his beloved Lake District. The Harrogate hoteliers also feared that the engines would frighten the grazing cattle on the Stray, and that the inferior incomers would bring their own food with them - and eat it in public.

However, the opposition was eventually overcome and, albeit kicking and screaming, Harrogate entered the Railway Age when the Church Fenton branch of the York & Midland opened on 20 July 1848 with a ceremony at the new Brunswick Railway Station, which was on the site of what is now Trinity Church Stray. The Leeds & Thirsk Railway Company's Leeds to Starbeck line followed just over a month later, but plans to link the two were dropped because the line would have to cross the Stray.

Did you know?
Betty Lupton
One of the characters of Harrogate at this time was Betty Lupton, the so-called 'Queen of the Well', who administered the waters with her long-handled horn spoon and cup for no less than 56 years. When she retired in 1843, she was uniquely granted a pension by the Commissioners, but unfortunately Betty died in 1845.

Stagecoaches were still being used to transport visitors around Harrogate in the early 20th century.

Victorian Harrogate 53

THE STRAY 1902 48967p

Seven years later, both railway companies were dissolved and incorporated into the North Eastern Railway Company, which obtained an Act of Parliament in 1859 to construct a more convenient loop line into central Harrogate. The problem was that the proposed line would still have to cross the sacrosanct ground of the Stray, and it was only the skilled diplomacy of Alderman Richard Ellis which made it possible. He suggested that the inadequate Brunswick Station should be demolished and the land returned to the townspeople as part of the Stray. The new line, which crossed the Stray in a deep cutting, opened in August 1862, with a brand new, brick-built central station on what is now Station Square.

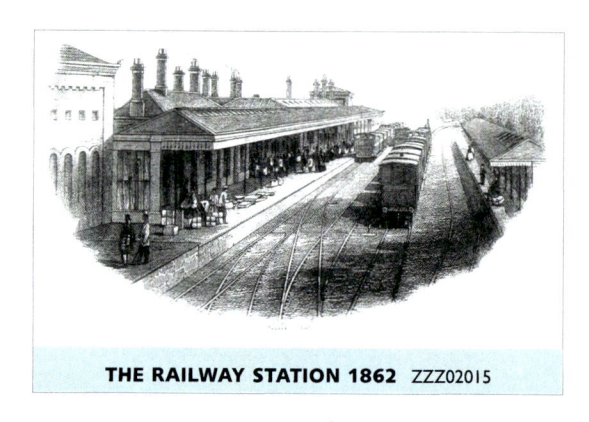

THE RAILWAY STATION 1862 ZZZ02015

THE RAILWAY STATION 2004 ZZZ02010 (John Morrison)

The modern utilitarian Harrogate Railway Station.

Victorian Harrogate 55

The Station Hotel (left) stands in Station Square opposite the Victoria Monument (right).

STATION SQUARE 1921 71649p

A railway porter stands by his wickerwork trolley outside the ornate entrance to Harrogate's Station Hotel, while pinafored schoolgirls look on.

STATION SQUARE 1902 48978p

HARROGATE – *a history and celebration of the town*

After water and gas supplies had been secured for the town by the respective Harrogate Water and Gas Acts of 1846, the next big impetus in the town's growth was the development of the fields which still existed in the centre of Harrogate between the High and Low parts of the town. The Victoria Park Company, which today would be called a development company, was created in 1860 with this sole objective. It was based on the original estate of the entrepreneur James Franklin, who had purchased a large tract of land there from Sir John Ingilby of Ripley in 1810. The elegant terraces of Prospect Place, Chapel Street and James Street were all his work.

When the Victoria Park Company was formed, almost inevitably one of its leading shareholders was Richard Ellis, and within the next three decades, the company oversaw the infilling of that gaping central gap based on the thoroughfares of Victoria Avenue and Station Parade. The new streets, consisting mainly of the more profitable retail and commercial premises, included Chapel (now Oxford) Street, Cambridge Street, James Street, Albert Street and Raglan Street.

By 1881, the population of Harrogate had risen to over 11,000, and leading townspeople like Ellis and Dawson were persuading their fellow Commissioners that matters like public health, and the provision of street lighting,

VICTORIA SQUARE 1935 87160

This view shows the gardens of Victoria Square with the spire of the United Methodist Free Church, built in 1865 but now demolished, in the background.

paving and sewers, were their municipal duty. It was a time of local government reform. Following a series of public meetings, it was decided to apply for Harrogate's incorporation as a democratically-elected borough council. The final public meeting held on 22 March 1883 was overwhelmingly in favour of incorporation, and the petition - 20 feet in length - was submitted to the Privy Council a month later and approved by the Government.

There were scenes of great rejoicing when the officials who had travelled to London to receive the charter of incorporation returned to Harrogate Railway Station on 6 February 1884; both Richard Ellis and George Dawson were among the many dignitaries waiting on the platform. The day started with a bang as the train arrived amid a barrage of pyrotechnics as the fog signals along the line were ignited one by one. Then a procession of carriages took the party through the streets to a dais for the inevitable speeches outside the New Victoria Baths.

The area covered by the new municipal borough was identical to that covered by the Improvement Commissioners, and excluded both the rural areas of Starbeck and Bilton-with-Harrogate. Among the new rights which incorporation as a borough granted to Harrogate were the powers to elect 18 councillors - six from each of the three new wards. The town's first mayor, Nicholas Carter, and the other aldermen were elected from among the councillors.

Almost immediately after the new councillors took office, a golden opportunity to purchase one of the most important sites in the centre of Harrogate arose. The Montpellier estate, including the Montpellier Baths, came on the market. It was purchased initially by George Dawson, who had foreseen the strategic importance of the site, and he re-sold it to the new Corporation in 1888.

The scene was set for Richard Ellis's fondly held dream of an international-standard hydropathic establishment for the town to come true, and the foundation stone for the new Royal Baths was laid on 10 July 1894 by the new mayor, Alderman Charles Fortune. The new building was designed by the London architects Baggalley and Bristowe, and it achieved everything that Ellis had hoped for in the quality and standard of the facilities which were provided. It was opened by the Duke of Cambridge on 23 July 1897 amid scenes of great rejoicing.

The building was fitted out in the greatest luxury, with polished marble pillars and floors, ornate plasterwork with classical inscriptions, and palm plants in abundance. The Turkish baths (recently subject to a £1million refurbishment) offered an exotic taste of the Orient, and there were a number of different types of baths and 'pulverisation' (presumably massage) and inhalation rooms. Naturally, Harrogate's efficacious waters were used exclusively in the new baths. Among the weird and wonderful treatments available to visitors in the opulent building were Aix-douche massages, Schnee baths, Greville baths, external douches, intestinal lavage, cataphoresis, and the dangerous-sounding static shocks and inhalation of radioactive gases.

The Royal Baths

A coach and horse waits outside Harrogate's palatial Royal Baths in the year of its opening by the Duke of Cambridge in 1897. Designed by the London architects Baggalley and Bristowe, no expense was spared with this sumptuous building to give Harrogate the latest, state-of-the-art hydropathic establishment, rivalling anything in other spas throughout the world. The roof even had special devices designed to melt the snow in the bitter north Yorkshire winter!

THE NEW BATHS 1897 39430

Victorian Harrogate 59

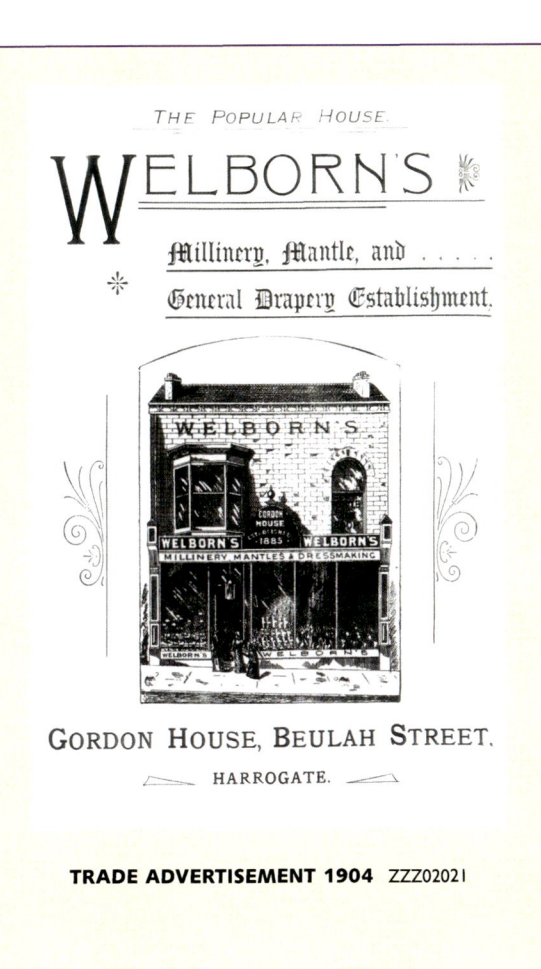

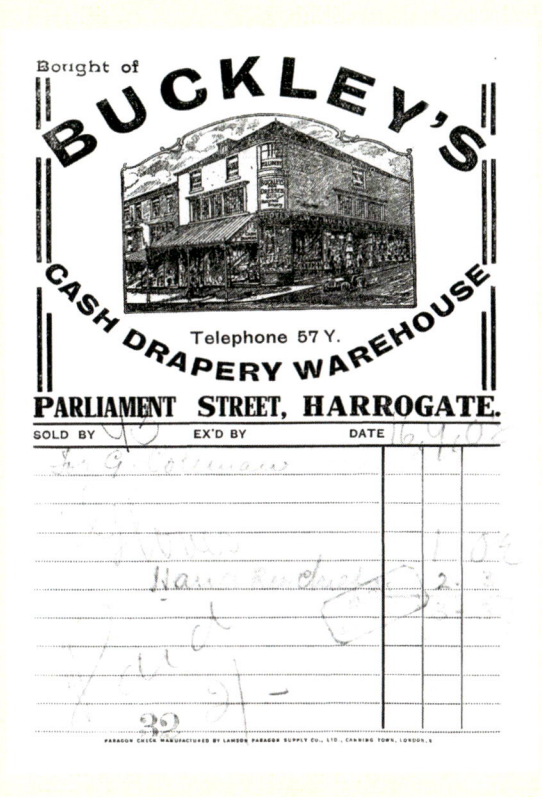

TRADE ADVERTISEMENT 1904 ZZZ02021

DRAPER'S BILL 1908 ZZZ02024

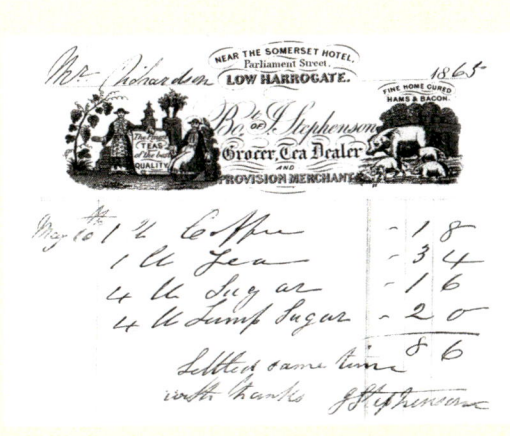

DRAPER'S BILL 1889 ZZZ02023

GROCER'S BILL 1865 ZZZ02025

Under the Local Government Act of 1888, Harrogate's civic boundaries were extended in 1900 to take in Starbeck, Bilton and most of Pannal to the south. This immediately had the effect of increasing the town's population from around 20,000 to 27,650, and the town already occupied the premier position among spas in the British empire and was ready to challenge those on the Continent and elsewhere. Thorpe's 'Illustrated Guide to Harrogate', published locally in 1886, proudly declared: 'Harrogate stands pre-eminent to all other places in Europe for the diversity and variety of its mineral springs. Nowhere else are mineral waters found in one locality so admirably adapted to meet and conquer disease in so wide a range of form, degree, and character', while Black's 'Guide to the County of York', published in the same year, again pointed out the unique situation of the town: 'The distinguishing peculiarity of Harrogate, especially High Harrogate, which is the more fashionable part of the town, is its complete openness to the sunshine and the green fields. A broad, unenclosed tract of land (the Stray) stretches in front of the main line of houses. This ground is secured by Act of Parliament (1770) from ever being built on; provision being thus made for preserving the freshness and charm of a rural position and prospect, in conjunction with all the appliances and advantages of the most aristocratic and artificial life.'

By this time, Harrogate had really begun to establish itself, especially among the rich and famous, and it was said that so many eminent statesmen were among its visitors that Queen Victoria could have held a cabinet meeting there if she had wished. As it was, the Queen Empress never actually visited Harrogate herself at any time during her 64-year reign.

The Victorians knew that protection was necessary against the harmful rays of the sun, as this photograph taken on the Stray shows.

THE PROSPECT HOTEL 1891 28307

Victorian Harrogate 61

STATION SQUARE 1911 63520p

HARROGATE – *a history and celebration of the town*

STATION SQUARE 1921 71649p

Victorian Harrogate 63

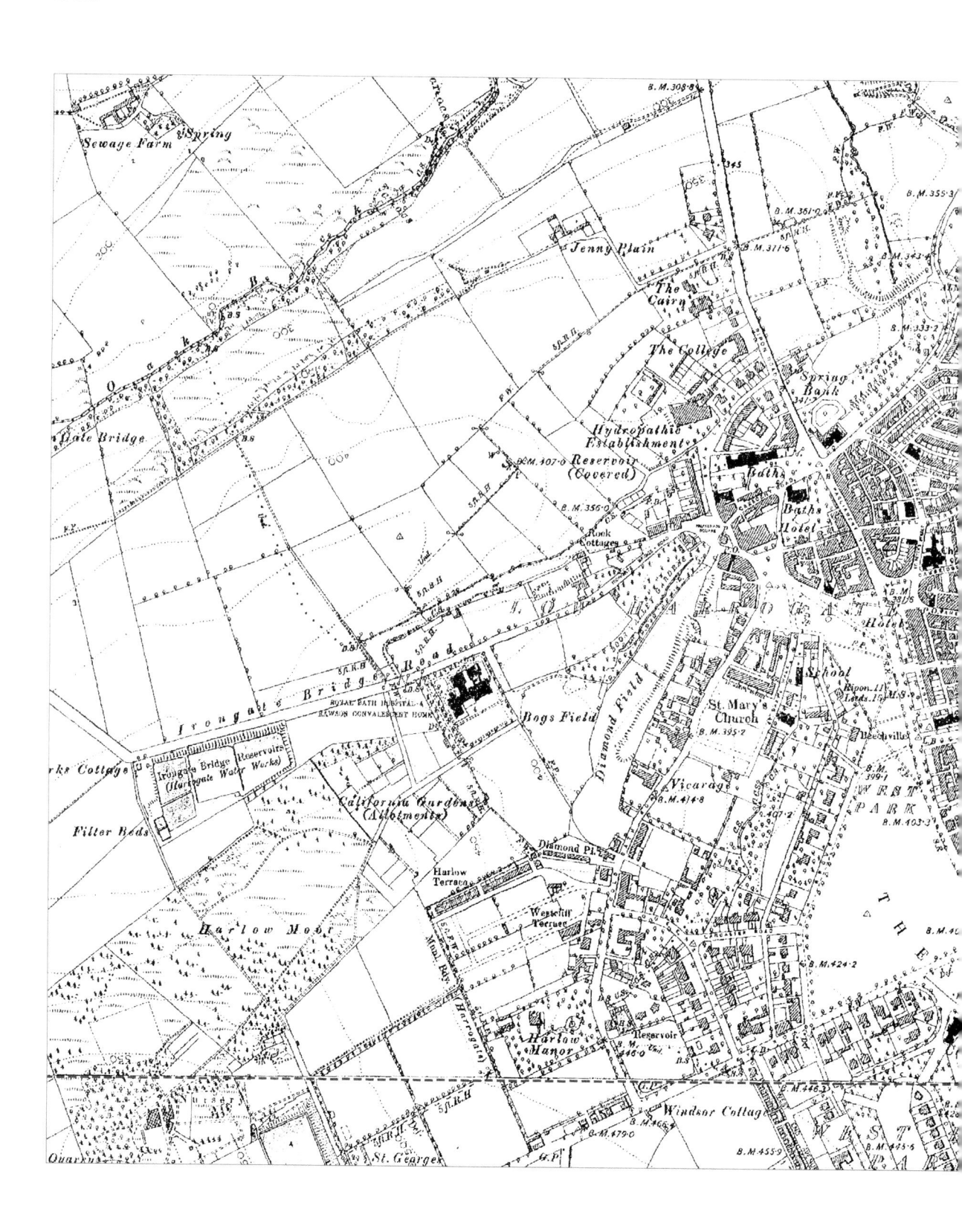

64 HARROGATE – *a history and celebration of the town*

Victorian Harrogate 65

HARROGATE ORDNANCE SURVEY MAP 1883-1890

ROYAL PUMP ROOM 1911   63522t

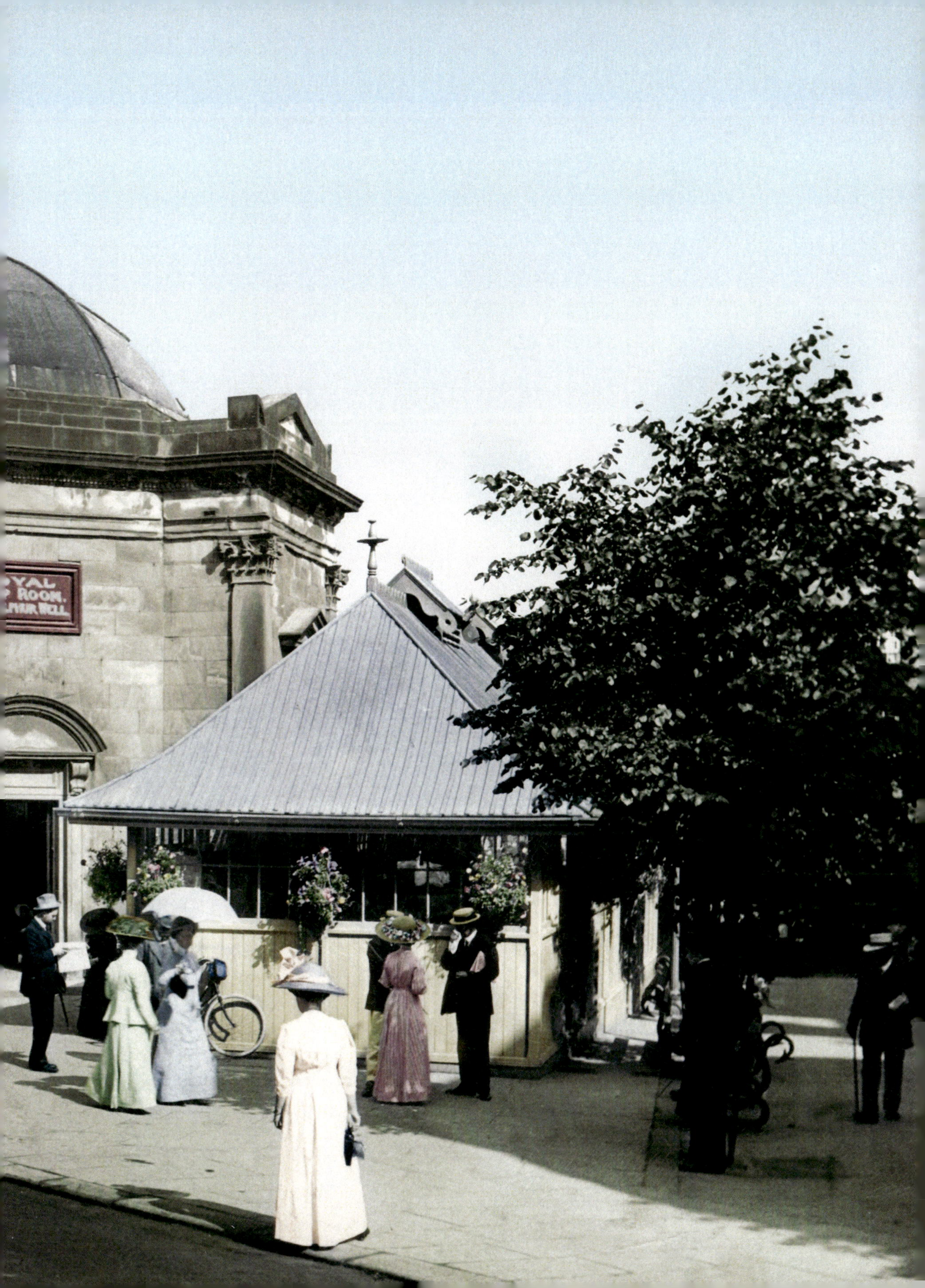
YAL
ROOM.

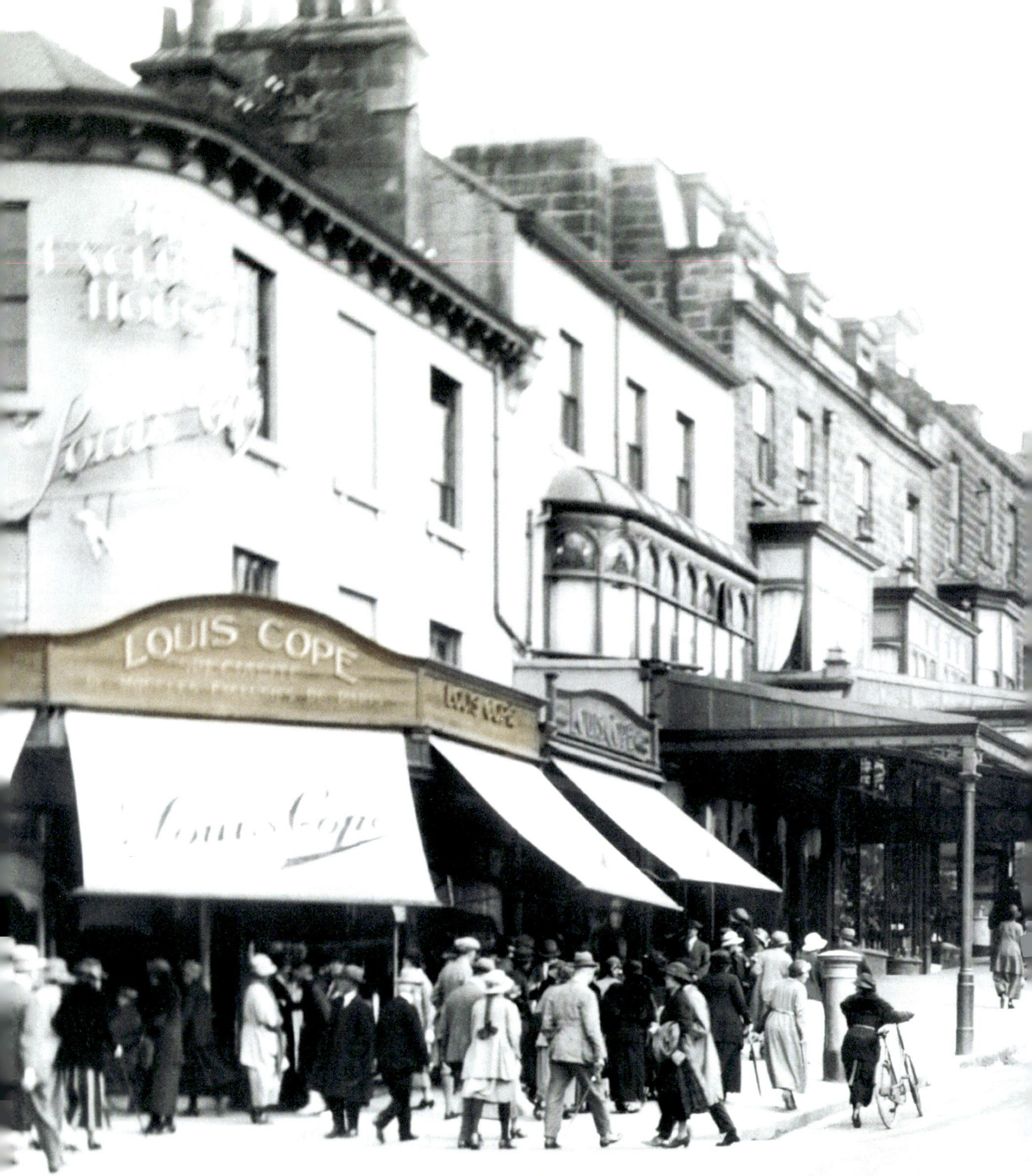
LOUIS COPE
Louis Cope

CHAPTER FOUR

The Twentieth Century

THE MAYOR'S BALL 1903 ZZZ02018

TRADE ADVERTISEMENT 1903 ZZZ02022

The Mayor's Ball was held at the opening of the Kursaal in 1903.

'A PALACE of gold glittering light, softened by distance to a mirage of creams. High in the limitations of space looms a patch of blue sky studied with gleaming stars of gold. Their radiance penetrates a succession of balconies with angularities relieved by architecture rich in design, glowing in creams and glinting with gold'. That was the breathless, slightly over-the-top description applied by a reporter of the 'Harrogate Advertiser' in May 1903 to Frank Matcham's auditorium in Harrogate's newly-completed Royal Hall, then known as the Kursaal.

The 'Advertiser' had rushed out a special illustrated supplement to mark the auspicious occasion, and the hyperbole went unrestrained as the journalists heaped praise on the sumptuous new building. The opening was performed by Sir Hubert Parry, the composer, conductor and director of the Royal College of Music, who later conducted the opening concert with the baton specially presented to him for the occasion.

The Kursaal - the name came about when a fact-finding tour of Europe found such 'Cure Halls' were a popular addition to the attractions of spas on the Continent - was breathtaking in its opulence. In addition to the heavily gilded 1,300-seat main hall, it included a 360-degree ambulatory and a fully

The Twentieth Century 71

KURSAAL 1907 58657

Frank Matcham's magnificent gilded auditorium in the Kursaal.

THE KURSAAL 1907 58656

The exterior of the Kursaal shortly after its opening.

glazed extension known as the Spa Rooms. It was renamed the Royal Hall at the height of the anti-German feeling during the First World War, but the name 'Kursaal' remains in the stonework above the entrance.

After the closure of High Harrogate's old Georgian theatre in 1830, the town had been left without a venue for theatrical entertainment, but this had partly been filled by the construction of the Royal Opera House in what is now Oxford Street in January 1900. Designed by J P Briggs, it also seated around 1,300 in an opulent auditorium and is now known as the Harrogate Theatre.

With the opening of the Kursaal three years later, Harrogate was becoming something of a cultural centre for the north, and such big names as Dame Nellie Melba, Sarah Bernhardt, Clara Butt, Lily Langtry and George Robey appeared on its stages. Many of these stars were brought to Harrogate by the impresario and conductor of the Harrogate Municipal Orchestra, Julian Clifford. He was responsible for first inviting Sir Edward Elgar to Harrogate, and he became a frequent visitor, noting rather sniffily that 'Harrogate thinks itself very fashionable and more than a little chic, and the ladies dress up terribly'. His Second Symphony was given its first provincial performance by the Harrogate Municipal Orchestra under Clifford in 1911, and Elgar himself conducted many concerts in the Kursaal Hall. His last visit was made in 1927.

THE KURSAAL 1911 63527

In 1911, people were still arriving at the Kursaal by horse-drawn coach.

THE ROYAL HALL 2004 ZZZ01991 (John Morrison)

The Royal Hall, formerly the Kursaal, as it looks today.

Musicians were not the only distinguished visitors, and in the same year of the Elgar provincial premiere, the Harrogate season saw visits by Queen Alexandra, Empress Marie of Russia, Queen Amelie and King Manuel of Portugal (these three all on one day), Princess Victoria, Prince Henry of Russia, and Prince Christopher of Greece. Harrogate was becoming a truly international venue, and members of the nobility made sure that a visit to the spa was firmly part of their social calendar, conveniently linked to their journeys north for the grouse shooting in Yorkshire or Scotland.

All these well-to-do visitors demanded the highest quality accommodation, of course, so in the early years of the 20th century there was a boom in high-class hotel building which was seldom to be matched anywhere in Britain. The building which still dominates the town was the 400-bed Hotel Majestic (fondly known locally as simply 'Number One, Harrogate', or less reverently as 'the Magic Stick'). The massive six-storey, copper-domed building opened its doors in July 1900, having been built in the remarkably short time of two years. It cost the developer Sir Blundell Maple a staggering £250,000, but it really was the last word in luxury. At its centre was the 8,000 square foot Winter Garden, heralded as the largest glazed space in Yorkshire. This was the 'delicious retreat' where, according to the Harrogate Advertiser, 'visitors can, on wet days, enjoy their usual walk under most happy conditions'.

In addition to the silk-panelled ballroom which was capably of accommodating 500 dancers, there were palm-dotted dining rooms and a smoking room adorned with 16th-century Egyptian panelling; the Majestic soon became the place to stay in Harrogate.

It was followed three years later by Alderman David Simpson's Spa Grand Hotel - later known simply as the Grand - with its six domes overlooking the Valley Gardens, which opened on 22 May 1903 - six days before the Kursaal had opened.

THE MAJESTIC HOTEL 2004 ZZZ01995 (John Morrison)

The grand front of the Majestic Hotel - also known as 'Number 1, Harrogate'.

THE PROSPECT HOTEL 1907 58642

The Prospect Hotel, seen here on the left, overlooking the Stray, was another fine hotel from the Victorian age, built in 1859. Originally known as Carter's, it is now called the Imperial.

The Twentieth Century

By 1911, there were no less than 800 shops in the town, and the population had risen to 33,700. With perhaps a heightened sense of their own importance, many leading citizens believed the time was right for Harrogate to have a 'Municipal Palace' to match its standing as a booming business centre and one of the world's leading spas. A competition held in 1902 for a Harrogate Town Hall was won by Henry Hare: his design for a suitably palatial building in Station Parade of 900,000 cubic feet featured a stately clock tower and cost £37,625. It would incorporate a public library largely paid for by the Andrew Carnegie Foundation, but in the event, it was only the library which was constructed, and it opened in 1906. When the politicians' plans for their 'municipal palace' were put to the public vote, they were turned down.

The last major ecclesiastical building to the erected in Harrogate was St Wilfrid's Church, which was constructed off the Wetherby Road between 1908 and 1935 in a solid, Norman style; it was much admired by Sir John Betjeman.

Because of the unprecedented demand at the Royal Pump Rooms (some mornings, up to 2,000 people were queuing to get into the building), a temporary extension was added in 1900; later, in 1912, a more elegant permanent annexe of iron and glass was built. The new annexe was formally opened to the public by the Lord Mayor of London, Sir Edward Burnett, who arrived in great pomp and amid much public excitement in his horse-drawn state carriage. The combined bands of the Yorkshire Hussars and the Mounted Police provided the music, and later a sumptuous banquet was held at the Hotel Majestic.

ST WILFRID'S CHURCH 1928 81541x

This is the northern aspect of St Wilfrid's Church, showing the crenellated north porch.

HARROGATE – *a history and celebration of the town*

This photograph shows the annexe newly opened by the Lord Mayor of London.

THE ROYAL PUMP ROOM 1914 67285

The Valley Gardens, first constructed as the Valley Pleasure Grounds in 1886, and the Crescent Gardens were extended and improved, giving visitors areas where they could both exercise and be seen promenading close to the facilities of the town. Entertainment was provided in these pleasure grounds by a variety of artists, including Tom Coleman and his white-faced Pierrots and Otto Schwartz and his smartly uniformed German Band.

Tom Coleman's Pierrots

This is a rare photograph of Tom Coleman's Harrogate Pierrots in action in the bandstand in front of an admiring Edwardian crowd in Valley Gardens. Coleman's Pierrots dressed in clown suits of white with white conical hats and wore the traditional clown's all-white face make-up. They played banjos and a hurdy-gurdy and sang many of the popular tunes of the day, to the delight of thousands of visitors.

VALLEY GARDENS 1907 58645p

HARROGATE – *a history and celebration of the town*

THE ENTRANCE TO VALLEY GARDENS 1914 67286

The Twentieth Century 79

80 HARROGATE – *a history and celebration of the town*

Enjoying Harrogate's Gardens

THE ENTRANCE TO VALLEY GARDENS 1914 67286
A newspaper seller plies his wares, perhaps with news of the Great War, outside the entrance to Valley Gardens.

VALLEY GARDENS AND THE TEA HOUSE 1911 63516
Edwardian ladies in all their finery enjoy the sun by the Valley Gardens Tea House.

THE CHILDREN'S POOL, VALLEY GARDENS 1925 78970
Children use sticks to guide their toy yachts in the pool in Valley Gardens.

VALLEY GARDENS 1925 78975 (inset)
Fashionable young things from the Twenties attract admiring glances as they promenade through Valley Gardens.

The Twentieth Century

THE PUMP ROOM FROM VALLEY GARDENS 1928 81526
This general view looks towards the Pump Room.

VALLEY GARDENS 2004 ZZZ02004 (John Morrison)
A modern view of the beautiful floral displays in Valley Gardens.

ABOVE: CRESCENT GARDENS 1902 48979
A view across the beautiful flowerbeds of Crescent Gardens looking towards the dome and entrance of the Royal Baths.

RIGHT: CRESCENT GARDENS 1907 58648p (inset)
Visitors in straw boaters and parasols gather round to hear the top-hatted band play in the bandstand.

82　HARROGATE – *a history and celebration of the town*

VALLEY GARDENS AND THE TEA HOUSE 1911 63516

The Twentieth Century 83

By this time, more than 165,000 treatments were being administered annually in Harrogate's various hydropathic and spa establishments, and at least 675,000 tickets were issued to visitors. The population had reached 35,000, and the borough held a housing stock of over 8,000 homes. In 1913, the 'Harrogate Advertiser' was as enthusiastic as ever in promoting the advantages enjoyed by its home town: 'There are many thousands of people in England who regularly turn their eyes to Harrogate. Their yearly visit to this famous Spa is the one thing that must never be omitted or postponed. Harrogate has become the vogue, not because it has practically every treatment that any single Spa on the Continent can boast, but because the people who flock here seldom if ever leave disappointed.'

But the storm clouds of war were gathering on the European horizon, and the exuberance of Edwardian Harrogate was soon to be dispelled as the actions of the Kaiser gave those loyal supporters every good reason to cancel their visits. Caught up in the wave of patriotism, thousands of young men rushed to take the King's shilling and recruit for the army. Harrogate was no exception, and the 5th West Yorkshire Volunteers - also known as the Harrogate Pals - was formed almost entirely of young men from the town.

Soon the pages of the 'Harrogate Advertiser,' the 'Harrogate Herald' and the 'Ackrill Annual' were filling with the names and photographs of the missing and the dead as they failed to come back from the killing fields of the Somme and Passchendaele. The towering white monolith of the town's cenotaph in Prospect Place, unveiled by the Earl of Harewood on 1 September 1923, records the names of over 800 of these young men, the lost flower of Harrogate's youth.

THE WAR MEMORIAL 1924 75634

Harrogate's monolithic War Memorial in Prospect Place is seen here a year after it was unveiled in 1923.

The Twentieth Century

PROSPECT PLACE 2004 ZZZ01994 (John Morrison)

A modern view of Prospect Place, showing the gardens and the war memorial.

Road Works

This is a glimpse of a slower, less pressured, way of life. Road works constituted no kind of traffic hold up in the Harrogate of 1914. This workman is busy with his pickaxe in the middle of James Street, by the Victoria Monument, as two long-skirted lady pedestrians cross the street and a coach and pair approach in the distance.

JAMES STREET 1914 67283

CRESCENT GARDENS 1907 58648p

The Twentieth Century 87

JAMES STREET 1914 67283

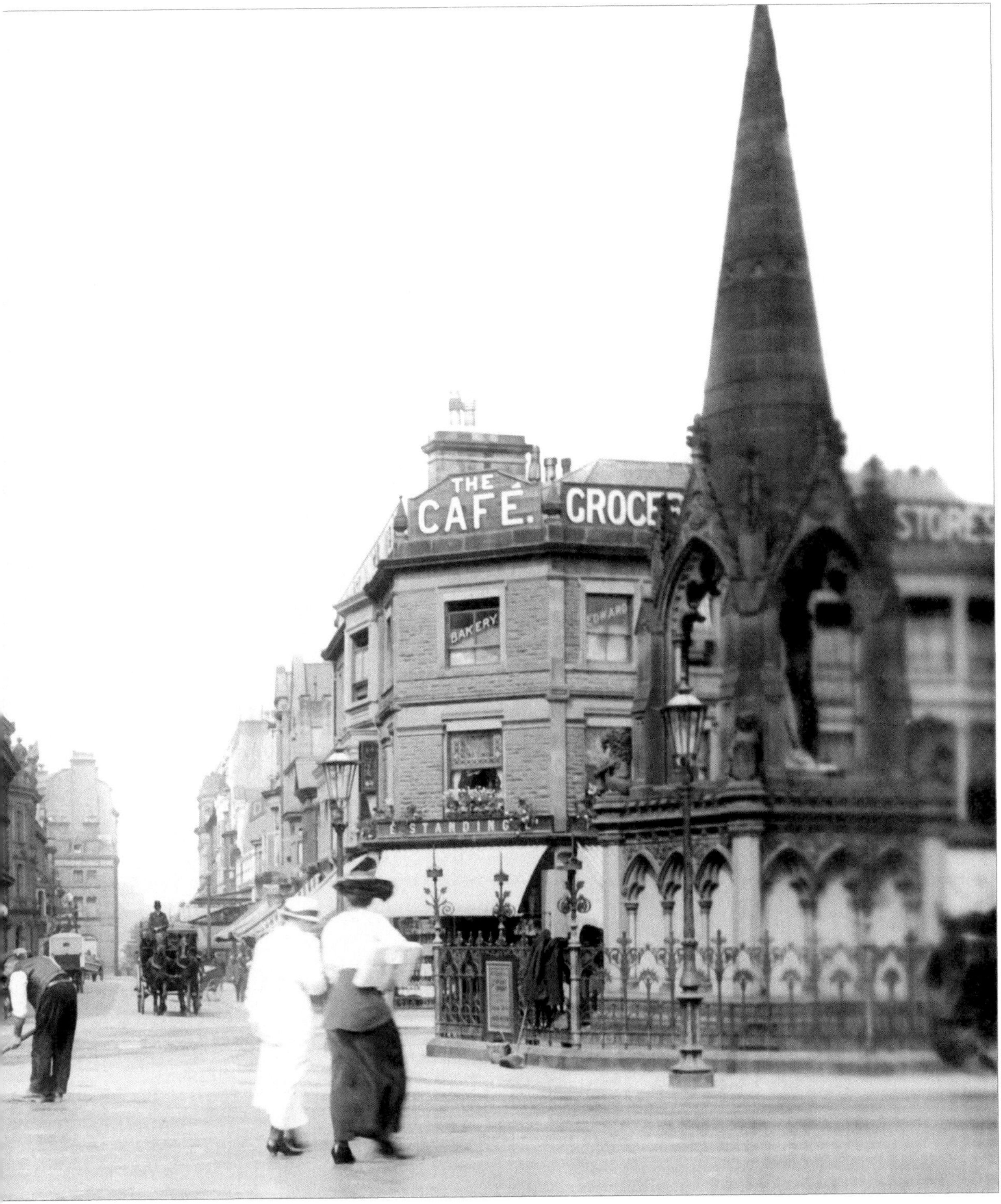
THE
CAFÉ.
BAKERY
STANDING

HARROGATE – *a history and celebration of the town*

After the war, the town was quick to realise that its Edwardian heyday as the destination of mainly the rich and famous was over, and a new middle class of visitor had to be attracted. Perhaps it was surprising that they continued to come in ever greater numbers by car and the improved rail services which were being provided after the war. Traffic and parking started to become a problem for the first time. The photographs show examples of the early motorcars to be seen on the streets of Harrogate. Picture 80223 shows a chauffeur-driven, open-topped car parked on West Park, and 75646 shows a pioneering lady driver parked outside the Adelphi Hotel.

ST PETER'S CHURCH 1927 80223p

THE ADELPHI HOTEL 1924 75646

The Twentieth Century

PARLIAMENT STREET 1923 74570p

Before the days of pedestrian-controlled traffic lights or zebra crossings, a policeman had to control the traffic at the foot of Parliament Street. But horses were still the favoured form of transport in the centre of Harrogate for some people.

Throughout the 1920s increasing numbers of visitors continued to flock to the genteel spa town, and in 1926 a record number of people used the Royal Pump Room. At this time, Harrogate was doing considerably better than most of its British rivals; indeed, a survey published in 1929 showed it to be the only one making a profit, with an income of £41,113 compared to Bath's £17,921 and Buxton's £10,000.

PARLIAMENT STREET 1907 58649p

THE ROYAL PUMP ROOM 1902 48974

An Edwardian couple leave the Royal Pump Rooms.

A Fifties family, with children in pram and pushchair, make the same journey over 50 years later.

THE PUMP ROOM c1955 H26127

The Twentieth Century

BIRK CRAG, CRAG HOUSE 1921 71656

Enjoying a quiet cup of tea in the gardens of Crag House, Birk Crag.

Agatha's Mystery

Agatha Christie's most famous mystery involved herself, and a secret trip to Harrogate in December 1926. The famous novelist went missing from her London home for 10 days, apparently troubled by the death of her mother, overwork, and problems in her marriage to Colonel Christie. It is alleged that she saw a poster advertising Harrogate on Waterloo Station, and resolved on the spot to go there. She stayed at the Swan Hydro, now the Old Swan Hotel, at the going rate of £5 10s (£5.50) a week, assuming the name of her husband's mistress, Theresa Neele. She appears to have enjoyed the varied social life that the spa could offer a young woman at the time. Eventually she was recognised and returned to her husband, whom she divorced two years later. The story was filmed as 'Agatha', starring Vanessa Redgrave and Dustin Hoffman, in 1977.

By now, the scene was set for yet another of Harrogate's ambitious and imaginative entrepreneurs to make an appearance. In 1928, Alderman Francis Barber, whose family had owned the Hotel St George, published his master plan for a 'cure park' based on those created by many of the European spa towns. Barber's plan was breathtaking in its scale and ambition. He wanted to demolish all the properties between Swan Road and Crescent Gardens to create a huge open forum and a 'drinking hall' worthy of 'the greatest spa in Europe'. Even in those days, the grandiose plans would have cost £1 million, and Barber had planned to maintain it all by the imposition of what he called a 'Kur-Tax'. The economic collapse of the 1930s saw to it that Barber's plans never left the drawing board.

The only effect that Barber's plans had was that plans were approved in 1933 for a 600-foot covered colonnade between the Royal Pump Room and a new Sun Pavilion in Valley Gardens, designed by the corporation's own engineer, Leonard Clarke. The spectacular circular dome of the Sun Pavilion used a special type of glass to filter out solar radiation, and the covered way meant that visitors could walk through Valley Gardens whatever the fickle North Yorkshire weather.

THE ROYAL PUMP ROOM FROM THE COLONNADE, VALLEY GARDENS 1934 86175

Tom's Bikes

This photograph of a Bath chair bicycle in Prospect Place is a reminder of 'Old Tom' Rochford, a well-known figure in the town during the early years of the 20th century. He was the first man to introduce to Harrogate the Coventry Cycle Chair, which was said to combine the comfort of a Bath chair with the mobility of a bicycle. Tom was known as the father of Harrogate's many Bath chair men; he worked in partnership with Sylvester Medici, whose brother owned a bicycle shop on Prospect Crescent. Among Old Tom's more famous passengers were the singer Madame Patti, the actress Ellen Terry, and the Duchess of Devonshire. King Edward VII also sat in Old Tom's chair and complemented him on its comfort. Old Tom died at the age of 81 in October 1931.

ST PETER'S AND THE WAR MEMORIAL 1927 80221x

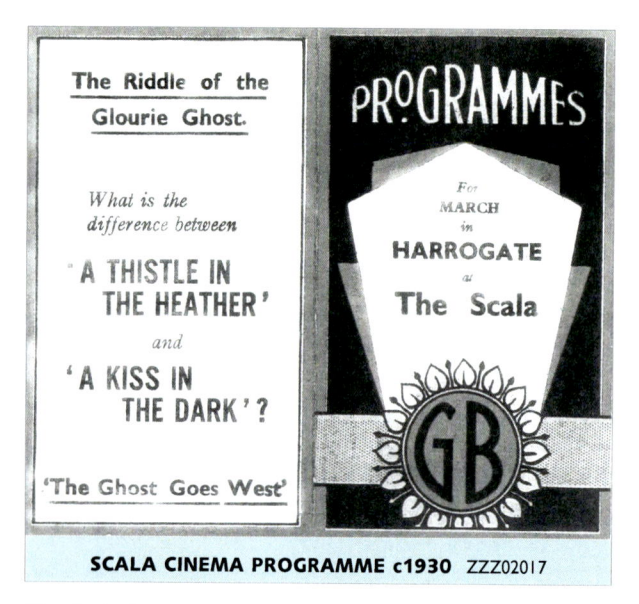

The Scala Cinema was demolished in 1962.

When the New Victoria Baths of 1870 were converted to new council offices in 1930, plans for Harrogate's grandiose 'Municipal Palace' in Station Parade could finally be assigned to the scrap heap. But the council were in trouble again in 1932 when they authorised the conversion of large parts of West Park Stray to flower beds and shrubberies. They had reckoned without the Harrogate people's jealous regard for their ancient rights regarding the Stray, and a Stray Defence Association was soon formed to express their disgust and anger at what the council had done. The Battle of the Stray had been joined.

The protesters quoted the 1778 Award, and claimed that the council's action was a clear and flagrant breach of their inalienable rights. At a heated public meeting held in the Winter Gardens in January 1934, councillors doggedly refused to listen to the complaints. The Defence Association immediately put up its own candidates against those who had voted against the motion to remove the offending flowerbeds at the next local election, and their election effectively won them the battle. The offending flowerbeds were removed in November 1934.

Less contentious was Clarke's 1938 extension to the Royal Baths by the building of a western wing, the replacement of the old Market Hall, which had burned down in 1937, and the opening of the bus station in 1938. Recalling the 1906 festivities, the Lord Mayor of London, Sir Frank Bowater, was invited to Harrogate to open the extensions to the Royal Baths on 10 July 1939. But it was to be the last flourish of those heady Edwardian days, as war clouds again threatened.

The exigencies of the Second World War were the only things allowed to compromise the inalienability of the Stray, and trenches were dug on the sacred open space during the Munich Crisis to deter German aircraft from using it as a landing strip. Old photographs show that during the war parts of the Stray were put under the plough and planted with corn to help the war effort. Much of the decorative ironwork which adorned public monuments such as the Victoria Monument in Station Square was taken away to be melted down for its precious metal.

The only hostile incident which directly affected Harrogate during the Second World War was the dropping of three bombs on the Hotel Majestic - the Luftwaffe believed it housed staff from the Air Ministry. None of the bombs exploded, however, although the conservatory was damaged and a villa on nearby Swan Road was demolished (see box).

After the war, Harrogate Corporation was quick to realise that the golden days of the town as a spa for not only the rich and famous but - with the advent of the National Health Service - anyone else as well, were well and truly over. In fact, the town undoubtedly benefited from the post-war Labour Government's Health Service, and it became the country's largest centre for research into rheumatic diseases when half of the Royal Bath Hospital was converted into a research clinic, with the Crown and White Hart Hotels serving as annexes for more mobile patients. The 'cure' had become the property of the nation, and by 1959, 80 per cent of the patients received their treatment on the National Health Service.

But Harrogate's city fathers knew its future lay elsewhere and, to their credit, they began the long and sometimes painful process of reinventing the town to suit the fast-changing world of the latter half of the 20th century.

The emphasis of the town's tourist advertising changed from its being described as 'The Queen of the Inland Spas' to 'Britain's Floral Resort', in recognition of its fine parks and gardens. The first Northern Antique Dealers Fair took place in the Royal Bath Assembly Rooms in 1950. This was the kind of event which was to become the town's new lifeblood, and the event now attracts over 10,000 visitors every April.

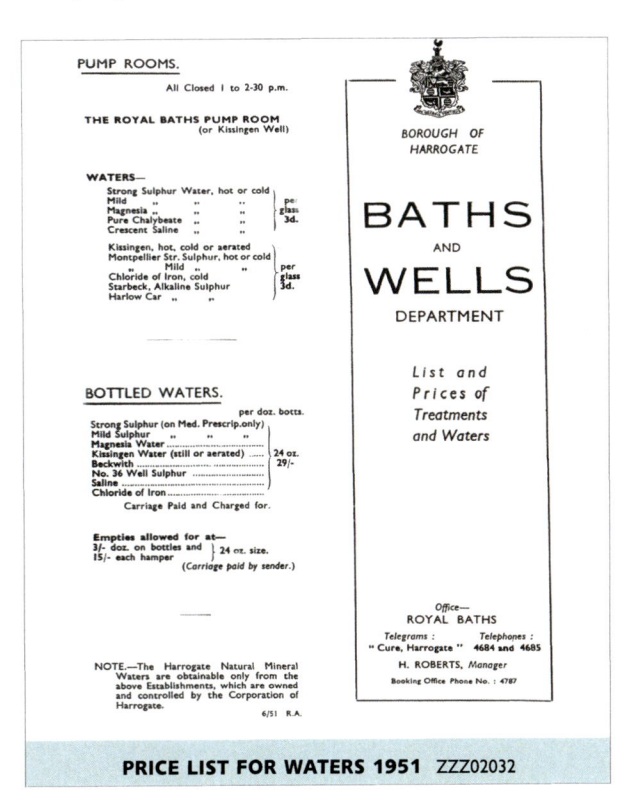

Did you know?
Bombshell at the Majestic
The unexploded bomb which landed on the Hotel Majestic on 12 September 1940 was found standing upright in an upstairs room by soldiers sent to investigate. At first, Captain G H Yates and Eric Stirk mistook it for a water tank, and they used the hotel lift to take it out. After the bomb had been safely defused, the casing was used to raise money for the Harrogate Spitfire Fund. Captured German documents revealed that the Germans had believed that the hotel was being used by the Air Ministry, but a newspaper claimed at the time that the pilot had once been refused a table at the Majestic's restaurant when he had called before the war.

PRICE LIST FOR WATERS 1951 ZZZ02032

The huge success of the 1951 Festival of Britain on London's South Bank did not go unnoticed, and the 'Yorkshire Observer' was able to report that year that Harrogate had hosted no fewer than 107 conferences, attracting a total of 44,325 visitors to the town. By 1960, this figure had risen to 180 conferences, which, it was estimated, boosted the local economy to the tune of around £600,000. The writing was on the wall. A sign of things to come, the town's first custom-built exhibition hall was erected on the Spa Room Gardens in 1959, and its immediate success pointed the way to a gradual extension of these facilities by the erection of additional halls in 1966, 1971, 1981, 1994 and 2001.

By 1971, the council was convinced that if it was to continue to benefit from the lucrative exhibition and conference market, it needed a new conference hall and hotel. Plans for a 2,000-seat conference hall, office block, shopping centre, 226-bed hotel with an underground car park, plus a further 20,000 square feet of exhibition space, were approved, at an estimated cost of £7.8 million. The final cost - to the horror of ratepayers - rose to £34 million, of which £25.5 million were building costs and £2 million legal and settlement costs. In 1988, the council leader ruefully commented that a project which had started out as taking two and a half years and costing £6 million to build had 'rocketed into space', taking twice as long to build and costing over four times the original estimate.

However, the controversial new International Conference Centre opened in King's Road on 20 February 1982 with a performance of Edward Elgar's 'Dream of Gerontius'. One wonders what Elgar himself might have thought about Harrogate's continuing attempts to appear chic and fashionable.

The success of the new Conference Centre cannot be denied. It regularly hosts major party political conferences, and also, in the year of its opening and in sharp contrast to the Elgar concert, it hosted the 1982 Eurovision Song Contest. By 1996, the annual value of the town's conference and exhibition business was put at £91 million - ranking it third behind only London, with Earl's Court, Olympia and Wembley, and Birmingham, with its National Exhibition Centre.

Outdoor exhibitions were also catered for at the Great Yorkshire Show's 100-acre permanent showground off the Wetherby Road just outside the town. The site for the permanent showground was first acquired by the Yorkshire Agricultural Society in 1950, and since then over £10 million has been spent on modernising and restructuring the site. Today, the three-day event has over 1,000 exhibitors and attracts over 125,000 people from all over the country as one of the top farming shows in the country. The famous Harrogate Spring Flower Show, first held in the Valley Gardens in 1927, was moved to a new site on the showground in 1996, and now caters for about 60,000 visitors.

During the Sixties, new industry also started to be attracted to the town, such as ICI's Fibre Division, the Post Office Savings Bank, the Mercantile Credit Company, and Dunlopillo at Pannal. This provided Harrogate with a much wider employment base than it had ever had before. Harrogate had always been the home of high-class shopping, but with the opening of the elegant new Victoria Shopping Centre on the site of the old covered market hall in 1992 and the new Marks & Spencer store on the site of the Victorian Lowther Arcade in 1998, the town's reputation for 'retail therapy' was beginning to match its medicinal therapies of the past.

Harrogate was facing the 21st century with a well-established new role, and some of the old confidence was beginning to return.

VALLEY GARDENS 1925 78975

THE WAR MEMORIAL 1924 76534

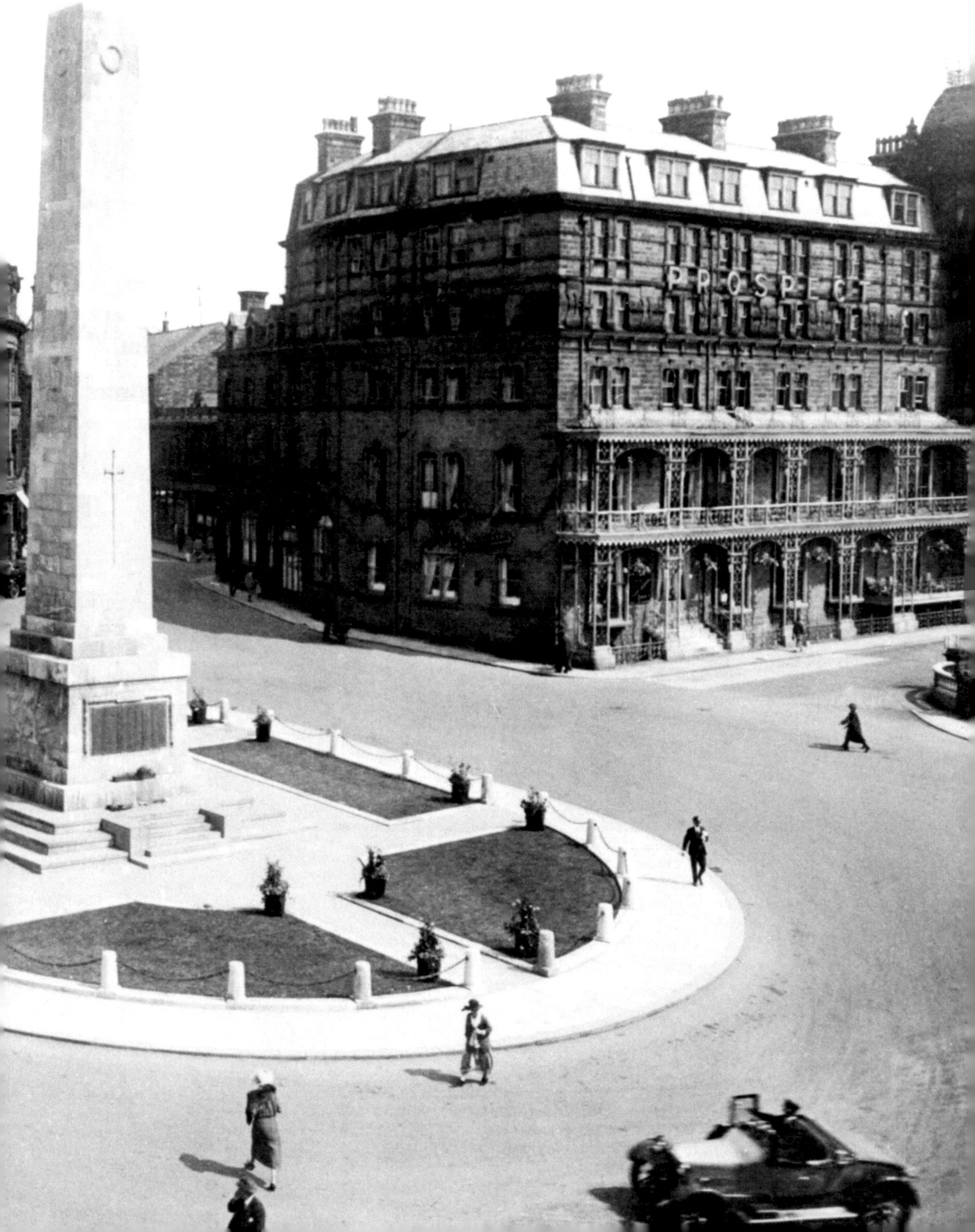
PROSPECT

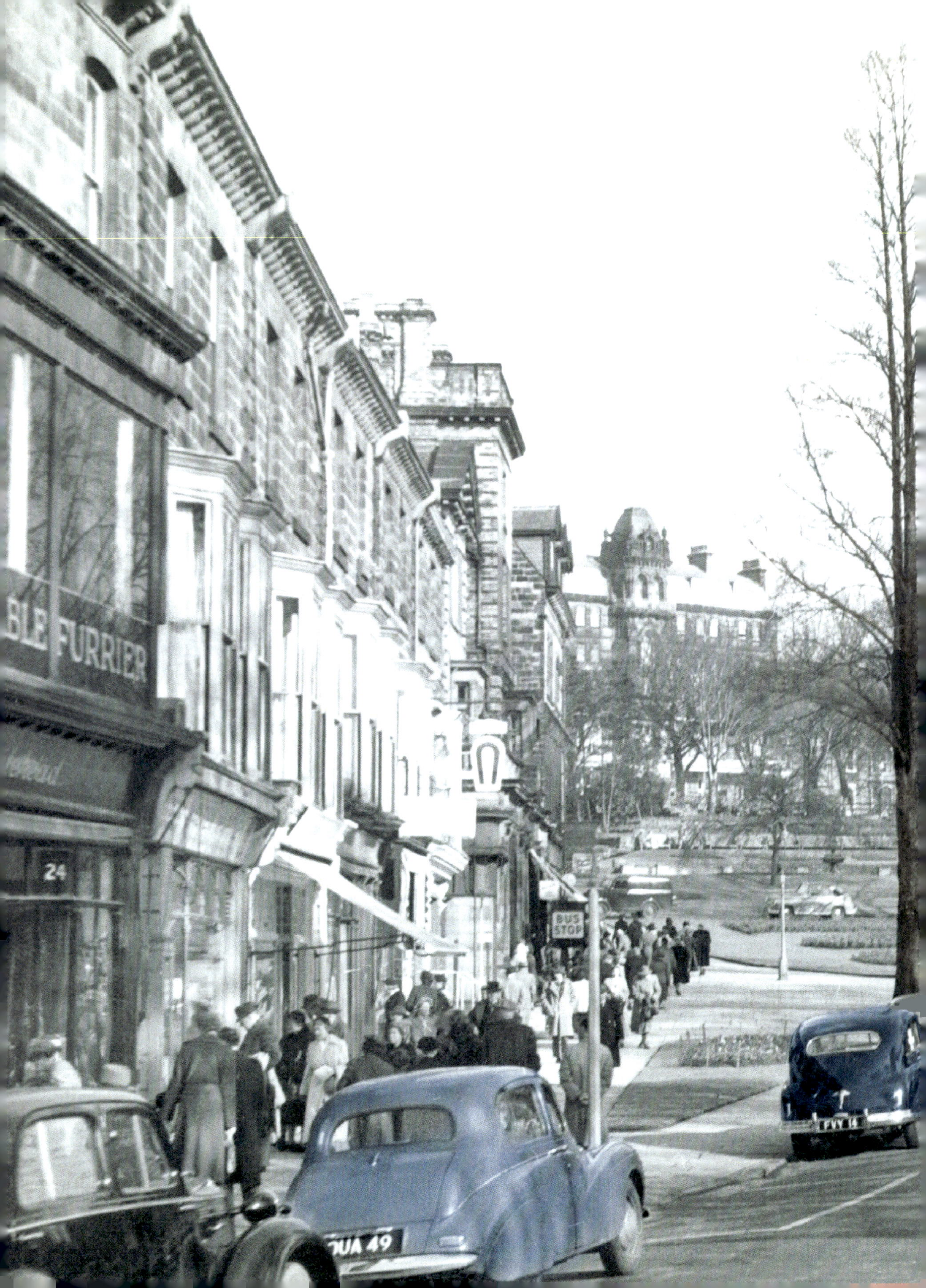
BLE FURRIER
24
BUS
STOP
FVY 14
OUA 49

CHAPTER FIVE

Harrogate Today

In the view of the Nidderdale-based author and historian Dr Richard Muir, Harrogate today 'embodies a strange blend of dowdy grandeur and yuppified vitality, the combination being made more wholesome by the retention of a Yorkshire grittiness and the keen climate from the upland winds which flurry and scurry across the Stray'.

That may be a little harsh, but there can be no doubt that Harrogate still retains its somewhat faded air of Victorian and Edwardian gentility which harks back to the golden years when it was Britain's premier inland spa, and the haunt of the great and good not only from this country but the Continent as well. Those days are long gone now, of course, and although 'taking the waters' is no longer the main reason for the thousands of businessmen and women and tourists now visiting the town, that genteel heritage is never far from the surface as they walk its streets and perhaps visit the Royal Pump Room Museum, the Mercer Art Gallery, or stroll through the Valley Gardens or on the Stray.

VALLEY GARDENS 2004 ZZZ02003 (John Morrison)

Modern sculpture in Valley Gardens.

Harrogate Today

Harrogate's elegant shopping streets are filled with cafes and bars and stylish restaurants offering specialist types of food from all over the world, while top class entertainment is provided by the highly rated Harrogate Theatre on Oxford Street.

THE STRAY 2004 ZZZ02001 (John Morrison)

Blossom time in one of the avenues which dissect the Stray.

> ## Did you know?
> ### The Coat of Arms
> *Harrogate's Latin motto, 'Arx Celebris Fontibus', immortalised over the doorway of the Royal Pump Rooms and in the town's coat of arms, is entirely appropriate: it means 'the city (or centre) famous for its springs'. It was adopted along with the coat of arms when the town become incorporated as a borough in 1884. The coat of arms also incorporates representations of two wells and two hunting horns, in recognition of the spa and the town's ancient origins as part of the Royal Forest of Knaresborough.*

Echoes of that past are still provided by the recently restored and re-opened Turkish baths in the Royal Baths Assembly Rooms. A massive £1 million refurbishment, helped by generous grants from the Heritage Lottery Fund, has brought them back to their colourful Victorian glory. Visitors can now once again 'detox' in the steam room, relax in the three hot rooms and finally take a dip in the plunge pool of Baggalley and Bristowe's 1897 arabesque masterpiece.

PROSPECT HILL c1960 H26130p

Traffic and parking were becoming a problem in Harrogate as early as the Sixties. Prospect Hill leads up by the side of the Stray.

106   HARROGATE – *a history and celebration of the town*

Another view showing traffic, this time around the Prospect Hotel.

ST PETER'S CHURCH AND THE WAR MEMORIAL c1960   H26122

Harrogate Today

The cultural highlight of Harrogate's year is the Harrogate International Festival, which was initiated in 1966 largely as the result of the work of Clive Wilson of the Harrogate Concert Society, with the encouragement of artists like the composer Benjamin Britten. Despite regular threats of the removal of Arts Council grants, it still continues to pull in the crowds for two weeks during July and August. The varied programme includes classical music, dance, jazz, the theatre, comedy, literature and crime writing, with the Harrogate Fiesta in Valley Gardens providing something for all the family.

Ever since its Victorian heyday, Harrogate has been famous for the excellence of its shopping, and in places like Parliament Street, James Street, Oxford Street and Cambridge Street, that reputation has been not only retained but enhanced.

> ## Did you know?
> ### Arthur Wood
> Arthur Wood, a former choirboy at St Peter's Church, sometime solo pianist in the Valley Gardens, and later deputy conductor of the Harrogate Municipal Orchestra, became a well-known composer when he moved south. Among his best-known works was 'My Native Heath', which was about his homeland of Yorkshire. The movement entitled 'Barwick Green' became better known as the signature tune for the world record long-running radio series, 'The Archers'.

PARLIAMENT STREET c1965 H26207

One of Harrogate's busiest shopping streets is Parliament Street.

Betty's Tea Rooms

No one knows for sure who the Betty of Harrogate's world-famous Betty's Tea Rooms was. The business began in 1919 when Frederick Belmont, a Swiss confectioner who married his landlady's daughter when he came to Yorkshire in 1907, set up his first Continental-style tearooms in Cambridge Crescent, opposite the tea merchant Charles Taylor's Café Imperial on Parliament Street. Three further Betty's Tea Rooms opened in York, Northallerton and Ilkley in the 1920s and 1930s, and Frederick built his own bakery in Harrogate to supply them. Eventually, in 1962, Taylors was sold to Betty's, and the present firm of Betty's & Taylors was born. But who was Betty? Various theories have been put forward, and the favourite one seems to be that the tea rooms were named after Betty Lupton, 'the Queen of the Spa' and manager of the Royal Pump Rooms.

BETTY'S TEA ROOMS 2004 ZZZ02009 (John Morrison)

The Harrogate of today is with some justification called the 'Antiques Capital of the North,' and the wealth of antiques retail outlets makes it a Mecca for collectors of all kinds of furniture, fine art and memorabilia. This interest, which is as international as was the town's previous existence as a spa, is also served by the massive annual Spring Antiques and Fine Art Fair on the Great Yorkshire Showground, when over 10,000 visitors flood into the town, and desirable objects are displayed for sale which are valued at millions of pounds. The Great Northern International Antiques and Collectors Fair takes place at the same venue in May, and another Antiques and Fine Arts Fair is held in October in the Exhibition Halls. Collectors come to Harrogate from not only all over Britain but from abroad as well, and the booming American market is always particularly well represented.

PARLIAMENT STREET c1960 H26207

Harrogate Today

THE VICTORIA SHOPPING CENTRE FROM JAMES STREET 2004 ZZZ01999 (John Morrison)

THE VICTORIA SHOPPING CENTRE 2004
ZZZ02002 (John Morrison)

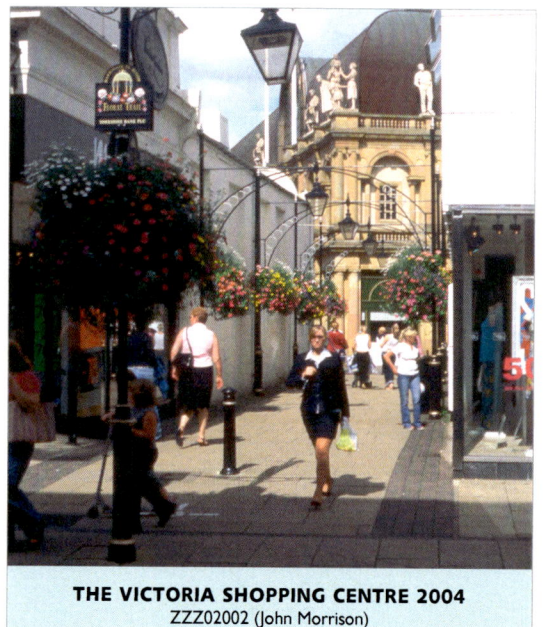

The opening of the new Market and Victoria Centre with its balconies and three tiers of shops and offices brought town centre shopping into the 21st century. Although some valuable older buildings had to be demolished to make room for it, at least it was in the town centre and not another of those out-of-town shopping malls which have severely damaged the city centre shopping of places like Sheffield. Marks & Spencer's gigantic new store is another prime asset to the commercial well-being of the town.

Harrogate Today 113

A detail of the modern sculpture showing the family on the roof of the Victoria Shopping Centre.

THE VICTORIA SHOPPING CENTRE 2004 ZZZ01998 (John Morrison)

MONTPELLIER HILL 2004 ZZZ02005 (John Morrison)

OXFORD STREET 2004 ZZZ01996 (John Morrison)

Smart shops line Montpellier Hill, facing Montpellier Gardens.

Oxford Street is one of Harrogate's most fashionable shopping streets.

THE INTERNATIONAL CONFERENCE CENTRE 2004
ZZZ01993 (John Morrison)

The ultra-modern frontage of the International Conference Centre.

Typically of Harrogate, there were many local people and businesses who predicted imminent doom and disaster when the International Conference Centre was built and opened in 1982. While it may well be true that the building project should have been better managed financially, there can be no doubt that the far-sighted vision which made it happen has been completely vindicated.

Harrogate now stands as one of Britain's premier conference and exhibition centres;

THE INTERNATIONAL CONFERENCE CENTRE 2004 ZZZ01992 (John Morrison)

A Tuscan colonnade gives a classical feel to the western frontage of the Conference Centre, facing Ripon

it attracts such prestigious events as the major political parties' conferences, in addition to many international exhibitions and fairs in the 16,500 square metres of exhibition space within the eight halls. A succession of concerts and other performances by top international stars also takes place in the 2,000-seat auditorium of the Centre.

By 2004, the town was attracting 347,000 business visitors annually, of which 190,000 were attending conferences and/or exhibitions, and 157,000 were going to trade fairs. The value of direct spending to the town of this burgeoning 'business tourism' was estimated at £160 million, while holiday tourism was worth £74.1 million. The estimated annual total of holiday and business tourists was 3.5 million. Together these two relatively new strings to Harrogate's economic bow were supporting the equivalent of about 7,000 full-time jobs for a population which in 2001 stood at 153,600.

With low unemployment (1.2% in May 2003 compared with the national average of 2.6%), higher than average incomes, and a top ten position in the national 'most profitable place to do business' league, Harrogate could justly be called a boom town by 2004. Average house prices in 2003 were 31 per cent higher than the national average, and 33 per cent higher than in the rest of North Yorkshire - not bad for a humble little spa town about which, only 50 years ago, the local writer Arnold Kellett sadly observed: 'The stately Queen of Inland Watering Places was painlessly slipping away into history'.

The best time to visit Harrogate is undoubtedly in the spring, when the still-inviolate 200 acres of the Stray bursts into glorious colour as the millions of crocuses and daffodils planted by the council come into bloom. It is a sight unmatched in any other British town or city, and eclipses even neighbouring York's famous clouds of daffodils below its city walls.

Harrogate's reputation as 'England's Floral Town' perhaps stems from the establishment of the Northern Horticultural Society's 68-acre trial gardens at Harlow Carr in 1949, where TV gardener Geoffrey Smith was once superintendent. Now run by the Royal Horticultural Society, Harlow Carr includes a beautiful streamside garden, a woodland arboretum, ornamental gardens, and several national collections of plants, along with plants suitable for growing in northern climates.

The first Harrogate Spring Flower Show was held in Valley Gardens in 1927, and in 1996 it was moved to the Great Yorkshire Showground, where it still takes place in April. The beauty of the town's meticulously maintained flower beds and displays is well-known, and in 2003, Harrogate won the coveted Britain in Bloom gold medal and was a finalist in the Entente Floriale, or Europe in Bloom.

The Stray, kept as a jealously guarded open space for use of the people of the town and its visitors for an astonishing 220 years, still lies as the green heart of Harrogate, and it is a facility which is the envy of many a larger city. It is probably only approached in its extent and usage by London's Royal Parks, but it is a fragile heritage on which constant vigilance has to be exercised.

HARROGATE – *a history and celebration of the town*

THE STRAY 2004 ZZZ01997 (John Morrison)

The precious escape provided by the Stray - a lone walker enjoys the solitude.

According to the respected local historian Malcolm Neesam, 'The Battle of The Stray' has to be fought about once every decade as it falls victim to the whims and fancies of whatever pet scheme a new coterie of councillors may come up with. In his 1989 book 'Exclusively Harrogate', he explains: 'Thus one councillor may have urged that 'temporary exhibition halls be erected on the Stray - they can be removed later and the grass will grow again'. Another may find that the entire traffic problems of the town may be solved by shaving a corner from Granby Corner Stray. Yet another may urge the construction of a huge boating lake near the Tewit Well. As in the past, so for ever should the public answer be 'not a blade of grass, not an inch of soil - the Stray is not negotiable'.'

Long may it remain so.

Cupid and Psyche

This white marble statue of Cupid and Psyche by the Italian master Giovanni Maria Benzoni stands in the Crescent Gardens (formerly known as the Royal Hall Gardens) in the centre of Harrogate. It is now sheltered from the elements by an ornate modern cupola, but when this photograph was taken, it still stood unprotected in a flowerbed, illuminated at night by floodlighting.

CRESCENT GARDENS 1925 78966

ACKNOWLEDGEMENTS

Anyone attempting to write a history of a town like Harrogate must rely heavily on the original research of many others who have gone before. I would like particularly to express my indebtedness to the work of the distinguished local historian Malcolm Neesam, and an old friend and the doyen of writers on Yorkshire, Bill Mitchell, on whose previous publications many of the facts in this present work have been based. Any mistakes, however, are the author's alone.
I would also like to thank another good friend, John Morrison of Hebden Bridge, for providing his (as always) excellent modern photographs of Harrogate; and Dave Lewis, who generously provided, at short notice, the examples of Harrogate ephemera from his wonderful collection.

DEDICATION

This book is dedicated to my beautiful new granddaughter Amy Heather, who was born during its preparation.

BIBLIOGRAPHY

Black's Guide to the County of York (1886), Adam & Charles Black.
Defoe, Daniel, ed Rogers, Pat - *A Tour Through the Whole Island of Great Britain* (1971 reprint, orig. 1724-27), Penguin.
Ekwall, Eilert - *Concise Oxford Dictionary of English Place-names* (1960), Oxford University Press
Grainge, William - *The History and Topography of Harrogate and the Forest of Knaresborough* (1988 reprint, orig. 1871), M T D Rigg Publications.
Haythornthwaite, W - *Harrogate Story* (1954), Dalesman Publishing.
Mitchell, W R - *Harrogate Past* (2001), Phillimore & Co.
Ed. Morris, Christopher - *The Illustrated Journeys of Celia Fiennes c1682-c1712* (1982), Webb & Bower.
Muir, Richard - *The Dales of Yorkshire - a Portrait* (1991), Macmillan.
Neesam, Malcolm - *Bygone Harrogate* (1999), Breedon Books.
Neesam, Malcolm - *Exclusively Harrogate* (1989), Smith Settle.
Neesam, Malcolm - *Harrogate, History and Guide* (2001), Tempus Publishing.
Patmore, J A - *An Atlas of Harrogate* (1963), Harrogate Corporation.
Thorpe's Illustrated Guide to Harrogate (1986 reprint, orig. 1886), Chantry Press.

FRITH PRODUCTS & SERVICES

Francis Frith would doubtless be pleased to know that the pioneering publishing venture he started in 1860 still continues today. Over a hundred and forty years later, The Francis Frith Collection continues in the same innovative tradition and is now one of the foremost publishers of vintage photographs in the world. Some of the current activities include:

INTERIOR DECORATION

Today Frith's photographs can be seen framed and as giant wall murals in thousands of pubs, restaurants, hotels, banks, retail stores and other public buildings throughout the country. In every case they enhance the unique local atmosphere of the places they depict and provide reminders of gentler days in an increasingly busy and frenetic world.

PRODUCT PROMOTIONS

Frith products are used by many major companies to promote the sales of their own products or to reinforce their own history and heritage. Frith promotions have been used by Hovis bread, Courage beers, Scots Porage Oats, Colman's mustard, Cadbury's foods, Mellow Birds coffee, Dunhill pipe tobacco, Guinness, and Bulmer's Cider.

GENEALOGY AND FAMILY HISTORY

As the interest in family history and roots grows world-wide, more and more people are turning to Frith's photographs of Great Britain for images of the towns, villages and streets where their ancestors lived; and, of course, photographs of the churches and chapels where their ancestors were christened, married and buried are an essential part of every genealogy tree and family album.

FRITH PRODUCTS

All Frith photographs are available Framed or just as Mounted Prints and Posters (size 23 x 16 inches). These may be ordered from the address below. Other products available are - Address Books, Calendars, Jigsaws, Canvas Prints, Postcards and local and prestige books.

THE INTERNET

Already ninety thousand Frith photographs can be viewed and purchased on the internet through the Frith websites and a myriad of partner sites.

For more detailed information on Frith products, look at this site:
www.francisfrith.com

See the complete list of Frith Books at: www.francisfrith.com
This web site is regularly updated with the latest list of publications from The Francis Frith Collection. If you wish to buy books relating to another part of the country that your local bookshop does not stock, you may purchase on-line.

For further information, trade, or author enquiries please contact us at the address below:
The Francis Frith Collection, Unit 6, Oakley Business Park, Wylye Road, Dinton, Wiltshire SP3 5EU.
Tel: +44 (0)1722 716 376 Fax: +44 (0)1722 716 881   Email: sales@francisfrith.co.uk

See Frith products on the internet at www.francisfrith.com

FREE PRINT OF YOUR CHOICE
CHOOSE A PHOTOGRAPH FROM THIS BOOK
+ £3.80 POSTAGE

Mounted Print
Overall size 14 x 11 inches (355 x 280mm)

TO RECEIVE YOUR FREE PRINT

Choose any Frith photograph in this book

Simply complete the Voucher opposite and return it with your remittance for £3.50 (to cover postage and handling) and we will print the photograph of your choice in SEPIA (size 11 x 8 inches) and supply it in a cream mount ready to frame (overall size 14 x 11 inches).

Order additional Mounted Prints at HALF PRICE - £12.00 each (normally £24.00)

If you would like to order more Frith prints from this book, possibly as gifts for friends and family, you can buy them at half price (with no additional postage costs).

Have your Mounted Prints framed

For an extra £20.00 per print you can have your mounted print(s) framed in an elegant polished wood and gilt moulding, overall size 16 x 13 inches (no additional postage required).

IMPORTANT!

❶ Please note: aerial photographs and photographs with a reference number starting with a "Z" are not Frith photographs and cannot be supplied under this offer.

❷ Offer valid for delivery to one UK address only.

❸ These special prices are only available if you use this form to order. You must use the ORIGINAL VOUCHER on this page (no copies permitted). We can only despatch to one UK address.

❹ This offer cannot be combined with any other offer.

As a customer your name & address will be stored by Frith but not sold or rented to third parties. Your data will be used for the purpose of this promotion only.

Send completed Voucher form to:

**The Francis Frith Collection,
19 Kingsmead Business Park, Gillingham,
Dorset SP8 5FB**

Voucher
for FREE and Reduced Price Frith Prints

Please do not photocopy this voucher. Only the original is valid, so please fill it in, cut it out and return it to us with your order.

Picture ref no	Page no	Qty	Mounted @ £12.00	Framed + £20.00	Total Cost £
		1	Free of charge*	£	£
			£12.00	£	£
			£12.00	£	£
			£12.00	£	£
			£12.00	£	£
			£12.00	£	£

*Please allow 28 days for delivery.
Offer available to one UK address only*

* Post & handling £3.80

Total Order Cost £

Title of this book ....

I enclose a cheque/postal order for £ ....
made payable to 'The Francis Frith Collection'

OR please debit my Mastercard / Visa / Maestro card, details below

Card Number:

Issue No (Maestro only):   Valid from (Maestro):

Card Security Number: Expires:

Signature:

Name Mr/Mrs/Ms ....
Address ....
....
....
.... Postcode ....
Daytime Tel No ....
Email ....

Valid to 31/12/16

Free Print – see overleaf

Can you help us with information about any of the Frith photographs in this book?

We are gradually compiling an historical record for each of the photographs in the Frith archive. It is always fascinating to find out the names of the people shown in the pictures, as well as insights into the shops, buildings and other features depicted.

If you recognize anyone in the photographs in this book, or if you have information not already included in the author's caption, do let us know. We would love to hear from you, and will try to publish it in future books or articles.

An Invitation from The Francis Frith Collection to Share Your Memories

The 'Share Your Memories' feature of our website allows members of the public to add personal memories relating to the places featured in our photographs, or comment on others already added. Seeing a place from your past can rekindle forgotten or long held memories. Why not visit the website, find photographs of places you know well and add YOUR story for others to read and enjoy? We would love to hear from you!

www.francisfrith.com/memories

Our production team

Frith books are produced by a small dedicated team at offices near Salisbury. Most have worked with the Frith Collection for many years. All have in common one quality: they have a passion for the Frith Collection.

Frith Books and Gifts

We have a wide range of books and gifts available on our website utilising our photographic archive, many of which can be individually personalised.

www.francisfrith.com

FF015340